Activate the Subconscious

Why Silence is the Greatest Success Strategy You're Ignoring

By
Jason A. Solomon, B.Ed

Published by Aussie Guys Books
ISBN: 978-1-7642115-0-5
Web: aussieguysbooks.com.au
Cover design, layout, and interior by Aussie Guys Books

"Delighting in silence is
a supreme blessing."
(From the 38 Blessings)

Contents

Preface

A Silent Awakening

I did not set out to write this book. Not at first. For years, I was simply surviving - teaching, raising a family, navigating the aftermath of personal losses and quiet breakdowns.

But beneath all that movement, something deeper was stirring. A slow, quiet voice that only made itself known when I stopped long enough to hear it. That voice was my subconscious.

The chapters that follow did not arrive fully formed. They emerged slowly, over the course of six years, during which I committed to the practice of silence, presence, and inner listening. These were not years of isolation, but of transformation. A transformation so subtle at times, I did not know it was happening until I looked back and realised, I was no longer the same man.

This book was born from that stillness.

The world trains us to look outward. To chase validation, noise, productivity, distraction. But the real answers - the ones that heal, guide, and empower - do not live out there. They live within, in a quiet and often neglected space we've forgotten how to access.

Activate the Subconscious is my attempt to map that space. It is not a self-help manual in the traditional sense. It is a lived manuscript. A reflection of the moments where silence revealed something sacred. Each chapter is woven from my own lived experience, grounded in daily struggle and spiritual insight, guided by experts like Dr Joe Dispenza, Brian Tracy and Cal Newport, and accompanied by other works I've written as part of my own evolution.

From losing my younger brother in a sudden car crash during my university years, to walking through the emotional fog of divorce, to quietly reclaiming a sense of self-worth without fanfare or applause - this book does not offer abstract theory. It offers a way of being. A return to the deeper voice inside that many of us have silenced for too long.

If you're holding this book, you are likely someone who senses there is more to life than what shows up on your to-do list. You might be tired of noise. You might be seeking clarity. You might not know exactly what you're looking for - only that what you've been doing is no longer enough. That is where my journey began too.

This is not a hero's journey. It's a human one.

And I've written it in a way that I hope allows you to see your own reflection within these pages - not as someone who is broken, but as someone who is finally ready to listen.

To listen to your mind, your body, your intuition.

To activate the brilliance that has been quietly waiting in your subconscious all along.

Welcome to the silence.

Welcome to yourself.

~ Jason A. Solomon, B.Ed.

Introduction

We are not suffering from a lack of tools. We are drowning in them.

Each day brings another hack, another app, another podcast promising a better life. But for all the talk of focus and flow, there is a deeper truth that most avoid - the real reason we feel unfulfilled is not that we don't have enough. It's that we've forgotten how to listen.

Our minds have become battlegrounds for attention, and in the crossfire, we have lost access to something sacred. The subconscious mind, that quiet and faithful servant within us, does not speak in notifications or hustle. It speaks in stillness. And stillness has become a rare and endangered thing.

For six years, I lived differently. Not by design at first, but by necessity. After personal loss, collapse, and a life that no longer fit, I withdrew into silence. What began as a survival instinct became a way of being. In those years, I learned to observe more than I explained. I learned that the subconscious isn't buried - it's simply crowded out. And once the noise dies down, what rises is nothing short of remarkable. Not mystical. Not dramatic. Just deeply honest. And honesty, when it returns, feels like oxygen.

This book is a record of what surfaced. Not in the language of gurus, but in the voice of someone who has walked through years of confusion and come out clearer, not because of more effort, but because of fewer distractions. Each chapter is an offering born of presence. Each one is guided by one of the 38 Blessings - timeless truths that grounded my healing and shaped my inner architecture. These blessings are not rules. They are touchstones. They remind us how to live with dignity, intention, and depth in a world that rewards reaction and speed.

As you move through these pages, you will notice that every chapter connects to one of my other works. These companion readings are not required, but they offer deeper layers for those who wish to keep exploring. Books like Shadow Work Demystified, 365 Days of SOUL, and Phobia Fighter emerged from the very stillness this book describes. They were not written to impress. They were written to survive, to understand, and eventually, to guide.

This is not a book to race through. It is a book to absorb. The subconscious does not respond to urgency. It responds to trust. And trust is built slowly, in quiet places, through repeated encounters with the truth. If you find yourself feeling exposed or tender as you read, let that be a sign you're getting close. Not to a finish line, but to yourself.

In our overstimulated culture, depth has become a rebellion. Silence has become revolutionary. But beneath all the productivity noise and performance metrics lies the same unchanging truth - your power was never outside of you. It was simply waiting to be heard.

Let this book be that place. A place where you remember what is already within. A place where you learn not just how to activate your subconscious, but how to live from it. Not one day. Not someday. But now.

Part I: The Science Behind Stillness

Subconscious Power

"Delighting in silence is a supreme blessing."

What if everything you need to know, decide, heal, or create already lives inside your mind, quietly waiting for you to turn down the volume?

The subconscious does not compete for attention. It does not speak over the noise or demand the spotlight. It waits. It listens. It stores. And in that unassuming patience lies its quiet power.

We are not taught to value silence. Instead, from the earliest days of childhood, we are conditioned to chase. To collect input, approval, data, answers, tasks. We become consumers of stimulation, mistaking busyness for purpose. More reading, more scrolling, more conversation, more connection, more doing. But amid all of that, we are rarely shown the doorway inward, where the deeper intelligence lives. Not the kind that recites or reacts, but the kind that already knows. It is there, buried under layers of repetition, noise, and avoidance. That quiet intelligence is the subconscious. And it only reveals itself when the distractions fade.

Before I came to understand this, I had unknowingly lived on the surface of myself. As a seasoned educator, I moved through each day with professional purpose and personal pride, juggling relationships, career demands, and parenting with a kind of mechanical resilience. I knew how to keep things moving. But when the external order began to fracture, particularly during and after my second divorce, something deeper was stirred. Not a breakdown, exactly, but a question. What if I had built an entire life on reactive energy, never really stopping to listen to the quieter voice beneath it all?

At first, I didn't know what to do with that question. So I did nothing. And in that nothing, everything began to shift.

Silence, I found, is not about sound. It is about interference. The absence of the unchosen, the unreconciled, the constant hum of input we mistake for thought. When people speak of finding stillness, they often picture a quiet room, a meditation cushion, a walk through the trees. Those can help, but they are not the goal. The real silence is internal. It is the moment you stop feeding the loop. And that kind of silence changes everything.

I began to notice how often I filled empty space. Podcasts during commutes. Television in the background while cooking. Checking messages while walking. Even reading, which I had always loved, became another form of input. At first, the silence felt awkward. It was like standing in an unfamiliar room where the furniture had been rearranged and I didn't know where to sit. But I kept showing up to it.

I remember coming home after work and choosing not to switch on anything. I would pour a glass of wine, sit outside, and simply watch the last hour of daylight slip into the edges of the trees. No conversation, no goals, no lessons. Just the faint hum of the breeze and whatever rose in me without effort. The first few weeks were thick with unease. My mind didn't want to cooperate. Thoughts jumped like static. But eventually, something began to settle.

It reminded me of a parable I had once read about a jar filled with water and soil. When shaken, the mixture turns cloudy. But if you place the jar on a table and leave it alone, the particles begin to sink. The water clears. That was my mind. Years of shaking. Years of being stirred by external pressures. And now, for the first time, the sediment had space to settle.

In those early months of silence, I was confronted with things I had long avoided. Past decisions. Missed cues. Emotional loops I had mistaken for personality. But there was also a surprising tenderness in what arose. Beneath the confusion and ache, I could feel something steady. Something alive and attentive. I came to realise that my subconscious had been waiting all along, not to correct me, but to join me. Not to criticise, but to help.

Brian Tracy describes the subconscious mind as a vast mental computer, recording every thought, emotion, and experience without judgment. It accepts everything you give it, whether accidental or intentional. It stores your fears. It memorises your patterns. It reacts long before you consciously decide. But most importantly, it responds to repetition. Whatever you feed it consistently becomes your default. If you offer it fear, it breeds avoidance. If you offer it chaos, it returns confusion. But if you offer it silence, it begins to clean. To reorganise. To prepare something new.

I didn't fully understand this mechanism at first. I only knew that the more I sat quietly, the more connected I began to feel to myself - not in a grand or mystical way, but in a grounded, deeply human way. I noticed small changes. I made better decisions without overthinking. I became less reactive in conversations. I started seeing my emotions, not as facts, but as signals. I moved slower, but more surely.

Brian Tracy once wrote that your subconscious begins to work for you after thirty minutes of uninterrupted solitude. At first, this seemed too simple. Surely it takes more than a half-hour to undo years of programming. But I tried it. Thirty minutes a day, no devices, no distractions. Just a chair, a timer, and myself. And gradually, I noticed something extraordinary. Thoughts would rise that surprised me - connections I hadn't seen, insights into why I reacted a certain way, long-forgotten memories that suddenly made sense in a new context. The subconscious, it seemed, was organising itself, offering me clarity I didn't know I needed.

The most remarkable part? It didn't feel like work. I wasn't solving anything. I wasn't putting in the effort. I was just making space. And the space did the rest.

We have been taught that transformation comes from doing more, fixing more, acquiring more knowledge. But I began to believe something else entirely. That sometimes the most powerful growth happens when you stop trying to manage everything and simply listen. Allow. Receive.

This insight mirrored the core idea behind my earlier book Shadow Work Demystified. In that work, I explored the hidden parts of ourselves that often drive our behaviour. The shadow is not inherently dark or dangerous. It is simply unacknowledged. And silence, I found, is one of the few tools strong enough to reveal it gently. The subconscious and the shadow are not enemies. They are both parts of us longing to be seen, understood, and integrated. In the quiet, they introduce themselves. They do not demand change. They invite it.

After about six months of this practice, something shifted. I no longer had to sit in silence to find clarity - it began to follow me. I could be in a crowded staffroom or a noisy family event and still feel anchored. I carried the silence with me, like an internal room I could enter at any time. I began making decisions from that place. I stopped chasing approval. I stopped explaining myself to people who misunderstood me. I began to choose alignment over achievement. Simplicity over drama. Presence over performance.

This is the transformation that silence brings. It is not just about mental stillness. It is about spiritual leadership. Your subconscious, once trained to respond to clarity, becomes your greatest ally. It offers guidance not through volume, but through resonance. You feel it when a situation is off, even if you cannot explain why. You sense when a decision aligns, even if it makes no logical sense. You begin to trust your own rhythm.

And perhaps most importantly, you begin to reprogram what you believe about yourself. You are not too far gone. You are not too late. You are not broken. You are simply full of noise. And noise can be cleared.

Silence is not a lifestyle trend. It is not reserved for monks or mystics. It is available to everyone. And it is free. The only cost is your willingness to stop. To sit. To listen. Even when it feels uncomfortable. Even when nothing seems to happen. Especially then.

You will not always get it right. You will have noisy days. You will feel restless. You will be tempted to give up. But if you keep showing up, something extraordinary begins to happen. The mind softens. The heart opens. The subconscious, long buried beneath reaction, rises like a tide you can trust.

You begin to live from the inside out. Not chasing. Not controlling. Just responding from a place of depth. That is where your power lives. Not in effort. Not in strategy. In stillness.

So take the chair. Set the timer. Turn down the noise. Breathe. Let whatever rises, rise. Let the mind organise itself. Let the truth return.

Because it will.

It always does.

Input Detox

What if everything you are absorbing is quietly shaping a life you never consciously chose?

It is easy to believe that silence is the absence of sound, but that definition barely scratches the surface. True silence begins not when the noise stops, but when the unnecessary input ends. It is not simply about being in a quiet room or walking through a forest alone. It is about creating mental spaciousness. About choosing deliberately what is allowed to take up residence in the mind, and what is politely but firmly refused. It is about discernment. And this kind of discernment is rare.

Each day we are surrounded by stimulation. The moment we open our eyes, the invasion begins. Notifications flash across our screens. Emails queue for attention. Social feeds hum with updates. News headlines scream importance. Voices - real and virtual - jostle for space in our awareness. Television, music, debates, podcasts, advertisements, updates, reels, commentary. A hundred overlapping conversations, and that is just before breakfast.

The world has become an all-day broadcast, and we have forgotten how to switch it off.

What few people realise, and what I only began to understand in the aftermath of personal crisis, is that every input we allow access to our awareness is programming our subconscious. The mind does not simply receive and forget. It receives and records. Stores.

Repeats. Acts upon. The subconscious is not selective in the way we might imagine. It does not filter based on truth, value, or meaning. It filters based on repetition. Familiarity becomes fact. Exposure becomes belief. What you hear often enough, you begin to internalise. Even when it is false. Even when it is harmful. Even when it is not your own.

Dr. Joe Dispenza teaches that your personal reality is shaped by your personality, and your personality is made up of how you think, act, and feel. Those behaviours and thought patterns are deeply influenced by your environment, which means that what you take in - visually, emotionally, and intellectually - becomes the scaffolding of your mental and emotional life. So if you are unhappy with the outer experience of your life, you cannot simply take action. You must address your inputs.

I remember a quiet afternoon not long after my second divorce. I had taken my usual spot outside, on a modest patio where the only distractions were a few wind-stirred trees and a distant kookaburra. There were no devices within reach. No music. No voices. No agenda. Just breath, breeze, and stillness. At first, it felt peaceful. But after a few minutes, the clutter began to rise. Thoughts that seemed to appear from nowhere, but had clearly been waiting. Half-remembered arguments. Imagined dialogues. A sudden urge to check the news. The memory of a social media post that had left a faint trace of envy. A half-formed worry about money. A tension that had no clear source.

It was like the lid had been lifted off a box I didn't know I was carrying.

That was the moment I saw, with a kind of startled clarity, that I had become a container for noise. My internal world was not my own. It was a collection of fragments I had unconsciously collected from a hundred places. And I had mistaken that chaos for thought.

This realisation changed everything. I was no longer willing to be an open channel. I had to reclaim my inner space.

Cal Newport, in his work on Digital Minimalism, describes our attention as a finite and fragile resource. He explains that the modern mind is not struggling because it is weak, but because it is overwhelmed. Like a room that has been over-decorated, over-furnished, and overstuffed, the mental space becomes uninhabitable. Newport warns that you cannot cultivate focus, depth, or peace in such a space - not because you are incapable, but because the environment is designed to keep you distracted.

I had always thought of myself as a capable multitasker. Teaching by day, managing a home, engaging in social circles, ticking off tasks, achieving, producing. But what I was doing was reacting. My thoughts were not intentional. They were fractured. My subconscious was not a focused instrument - it was a reflexive one. Responding to the most recent input, not the most meaningful one.

Newport insists that meaningful change begins with solitude. And solitude, he clarifies, is not simply being alone - it is being undistracted. It is the cultivation of mental space so that your thoughts have room to stretch, breathe, and return to their original rhythm.

I started small. I set limits on my email checks. I removed apps that added nothing of substance to my life. I stopped using my phone as a crutch for boredom. I walked without headphones. I turned down invitations that carried the wrong energy. I began seeking out input that nourished rather than drained. And slowly, something extraordinary happened. My thoughts sharpened. My mind cleared.

My internal commentary quietened. I found myself remembering things more easily. And most telling of all - I began to feel less anxious, even though my external life had not changed.

What changed was the quality of input I allowed.

Brian Tracy explains that the subconscious mind is like wet cement - impressions made early and often become permanent. Repetition creates permanence. So when you feed the mind a constant stream of superficial, negative, or chaotic content, that becomes your baseline. Over time, you build your identity, beliefs, and emotional setpoints around what was never consciously chosen.

Every time you hear that you are not enough and fail to reject it, your subconscious files it as truth. Every time you scroll through curated lives and feel lesser by comparison, your subconscious rewires what it means to succeed. Every time you listen to conflict-driven commentary or gossip-filled chatter, your subconscious embeds that frequency into your emotional field. These inputs are not harmless. They are behavioural scripts in disguise.

This is not hyperbole. This is how programming works.

The detox process was not glamorous. It was not aesthetically pleasing. It was raw. Removing the noise brought confrontation. Without distraction, I had to face the parts of myself I had kept hidden under the buzz. The urge to perform. The desire to be liked. The habit of constantly explaining myself to people who had no desire to understand. Even those interactions were inputs - emotional investments that did not return value.

I gave myself permission to stop feeding those loops. I stopped arguing with people who weren't listening. I stopped watching content that left me feeling inferior or inadequate. I stopped chasing updates. I even reduced the time I spent discussing certain topics, knowing that each conversation was either medicine or poison.

In that growing silence, I began to feel something unfamiliar yet profoundly comforting - ownership of my own awareness.

Phobia Fighter, one of my earlier titles, explores this exact mechanism. The fear-based loops we carry are often reinforced not just by traumatic experiences, but by daily repetition of anxious input. When we are not conscious of what we allow in, we strengthen the very fears we are trying to overcome. This companion reading offers a framework for understanding how the subconscious records, stores, and replays these patterns until we interrupt them with awareness.

What I learned during this detox was that the mind is not stubborn - it is obedient. It will follow whatever rhythm you give it. You do not need to cram it with affirmations or motivational noise. You only need to remove the false inputs. Let it return to stillness. The mind does not forget how to be quiet. It simply needs permission.

So I began to think of detoxing not as deprivation, but as preparation. Before a field can yield good crops, the weeds must be pulled. Input detox is weeding. It is the clearing of space so that your own thoughts can return. And they will. When the noise is removed, what rises is clarity. Creativity. Truth. Not the kind given to you by a guru, a screen, or a slogan - but the kind that lives deep in your bones.

I began to experience what I call original thought again. Ideas that were not borrowed. Decisions that were not reactions. A kind of slow but powerful knowing began to emerge. I stopped second-guessing every choice. I stopped rehearsing my worries. I stopped comparing my journey to someone else's highlight reel. I became still enough to meet myself.

And in that meeting, I recognised a version of myself that I had not seen in years - not the performative version or the one sculpted by others' opinions - but the grounded, quiet self who needed no audience. The self that had always been there, waiting beneath the static.

What you consume becomes what you create. And if your creations - be they decisions, relationships, or inner states - are not aligned, the cause may not be laziness, but overload. The mind cannot function when full. Just as a hard drive crashes when overwhelmed with irrelevant data, the subconscious begins to malfunction under too many unchosen inputs.

You are not broken. You are simply saturated.

Detox is not punishment. It is restoration. It is the act of returning your attention to its rightful owner. It is the daily choice to filter what enters, and to nourish what remains.

So close the tabs. Turn off the background noise. Walk without the phone. Cook in silence. Drive without a podcast. Let the music be the breeze, the breath, the slow rhythm of your own mind. Give yourself enough space to hear the thought behind the thought.

You might be surprised by what you find.

In that silence, you might meet yourself for the very first time.

Deep Work Reset

"Being devoted to a spiritual practice is a higher blessing."

What if the real reason you can't focus is because your life is built around distraction?

Focus is not a gift, it is a practice, and most of us have been practising distraction for years. We like to believe that our inability to concentrate is due to modern life - too much to do, too many responsibilities, not enough time. But the truth is, focus has become rare because we have made it optional. We have outsourced our attention to devices, platforms, and conveniences, and in doing so, we have forgotten how to work with depth.

Cal Newport defines "deep work" as the ability to focus without distraction on a cognitively demanding task. He calls it the superpower of the 21st century. But it is more than a productivity hack. Deep work is a sacred ritual. It is how we communicate with the subconscious mind and draw out its brilliance. You cannot tap into your inner intelligence if you are constantly being interrupted. You cannot build anything lasting when your attention is fragmented. Deep work is not just about getting things done. It is about remembering who you are beneath the buzz.

When I first began writing, it wasn't because I had something to prove. It was because I had something to clear. My thoughts were thick. Years of noise and trauma had built a fog inside me. I wasn't trying to be an author. I was trying to survive. I remember sitting down with no expectations, just a blank screen and a blinking cursor. I had practised silence long enough by then to recognise that something wanted to come through. I wasn't sure what it was. I just knew I had to listen. So, I wrote. What came out wasn't perfect. It wasn't polished. But it was mine. It was honest. And it felt like the first time I'd spoken in my own voice in years.

Deep work is often marketed as a way to get ahead. And it is. But the deeper truth is this: deep work is how you heal. When you sit with a task long enough to hear yourself think, you begin to uncover the parts of you that have been buried under busyness. You remember what it feels like to be present, to follow through, to give something your full self without flinching. That's not productivity. That's presence.

There was a moment, some months into this new practice, when I found myself watching my thoughts from above. It was subtle but powerful. I would begin to work on something meaningful, and instead of being pulled away by every distraction, I would notice the urge, acknowledge it, and return. This was new. In the past, my attention was like a leaf in the wind, drifting wherever life blew it. But now, I was choosing. I had become the observer of my own mental patterns. And that observation gave me power.

The more I practised deep work, the more I felt like a different person. Not because I was doing more, but because I was doing less of what didn't matter. This shift was visible even in my career. As a teacher, I had spent years juggling multiple responsibilities, often spreading myself too thin. But now, I could walk into a classroom with clarity. I knew what needed to happen. I was present with my students. And perhaps more importantly, I was present with myself.

The 365 Days of SOUL book series came directly out of my deep work practice. It wasn't rushed. It wasn't reactive. Each reflection was written from a place of presence, daily quiet moments that allowed me to speak from the soul. The process itself was as healing as the content. That is the gift of deep work. It turns creation into clarity.

Brian Tracy reminds us that the subconscious works best when we feed it consistent, clear input. Deep work is that input. It is the repetition of focus. Every time you return your attention to a meaningful task, you are rewiring your brain for intention. The more you do it, the easier it becomes. And this is where silence plays its part. Because deep work cannot exist without silence. Not just external silence, but internal stillness. A space where thought can stretch out, roam, and connect ideas without being interrupted by alerts or obligations. That space must be created deliberately. It will not arrive on its own.

One of the most powerful choices I made was to design my day around depth, not around tasks. That meant identifying the windows when I had the most energy and protecting them. No meetings. No casual chats. No aimless browsing. Just uninterrupted time with my mind. It also meant building in recovery - moments of silence before and after. Just as an athlete warms up before a race, the mind needs a runway for depth. I treated it like a ritual. And like all rituals, it began to change me.

You do not need to produce more to feel fulfilled. You need to connect more deeply with what you are already doing. You do not need to fix your mind. You need to clear the noise long enough to hear it. Deep work is not a hustle strategy. It is a healing strategy. It is the doorway to your subconscious. And the place where your true power lives.

Part II: Tools for Inner Rewiring

Habit Rewiring

"Living righteously brings personal blessings."

What if your habits are just rehearsed memories, and you've been rehearsing the wrong story?

The subconscious mind is a creature of habit. It thrives on pattern. It memorises what you do repeatedly, not what you intend, hope for, or wish, but what you do. And it doesn't ask whether those habits are good for you. It only asks: is this familiar? This is both the danger and the opportunity. Because once you realise that your subconscious is programmable, not fixed, then you begin to see that every habit you have can be edited, rewritten, rewired, but only if you bring it into awareness.

Dr. Joe Dispenza often says that most people live the same day over and over, calling it a life. We wake up and instantly reconnect to our past, same routines, same thoughts, same reactions. And in doing so, we recreate our personal reality from yesterday, again and again. This struck a chord with me because, for years, I had lived that repetition without knowing it. I believed I was progressing, after all, I was teaching, managing a home, navigating relationships. But beneath it all, I was repeating emotional scripts that had been written long ago. The same defensive responses, the same self-doubt, the same patterns of overthinking and avoidance. It wasn't until I removed the external noise and entered into silence that I began to observe myself more closely. I saw not just what I did, but why I did it. And more importantly, I began to realise that much of it wasn't serving the person I was becoming.

That realisation was confronting, but it was also the doorway to change.

Brian Tracy reinforces this truth: "Any thought or action that you repeat becomes ingrained in your subconscious mind." Whether it's brushing your teeth, checking your phone, or reacting with frustration, repetition locks it in. So I asked myself: what have I been repeating without reflection? It wasn't the big habits that revealed the most, it was the small ones. The things I did without thinking. The way I filled silence with unnecessary commentary. The impulse to scroll instead of sit still. The subtle self-judgement when I didn't feel productive. None of these were neutral. They were instructions to my subconscious. That's when I realised that rewiring didn't mean changing everything overnight. It meant becoming hyper-aware of the micro-choices and consistently choosing something better.

I started small. One habit at a time. Not with guilt or self-punishment, but with curiosity. I stopped checking my phone first thing in the morning. Instead, I opened a notebook and wrote whatever came to mind, even if it was just one sentence. I began sitting in silence before meals. Even thirty seconds made the food feel sacred again. I replaced evening scrolling with a walk, even around the block. That movement reset my energy in ways I didn't expect. I turned off all notifications. If something was important, it could wait until I chose to engage. These weren't massive transformations. But the impact was. Because each one became a signal to my subconscious: I am in control of my mind. Not the other way around.

In Shadow Work Demystified, I explore how unconscious habits are often rooted in unresolved emotional pain. We repeat what we haven't healed. This companion book unpacks how patterns of self-sabotage, fear, and shame are not just behaviours, they're learned responses embedded deep within. By bringing them to light, we begin the real work of rewiring. People often ask, How do I make a habit stick? And the truth is: a habit becomes permanent when it becomes part of your identity. It's not enough to meditate occasionally. You become someone who values stillness. It's not enough to journal now and then. You become someone who reflects. It's not about discipline alone. It's about alignment. When your habits match your values, consistency follows. And when your subconscious sees consistency, it begins to trust. It stops resisting change and starts reinforcing it.

Here's the thing most people miss: your habits are rehearsals. You are either rehearsing your past or rehearsing your future. For years, I was unknowingly rehearsing trauma. The same reactions. The same scripts. The same avoidance. But once I began living with intention, silence, and self-observation, I stopped acting from memory and started acting from vision. This is where Dr. Dispenza's work became invaluable. He teaches that you cannot create a new future if you are still emotionally attached to your past. That means healing is not optional. It's essential. Because your subconscious does not forget, until you show it something more powerful to remember.

Cal Newport reminds us that "environment shapes behaviour." If you want to change your habits, you must also change the places and triggers that support the old ones. So I began to redesign my environment. Not with expensive tools or complex routines, but with simplicity. I removed clutter. Physical clutter mirrors mental clutter. I replaced mindless entertainment with books and calm music. My home became a sanctuary for the mind. I created rituals instead of routines. A morning stretch with breathwork. Tea in silence. Evening gratitude on paper. None of this made me perfect. But it made me present.

Your subconscious is always listening. It does not speak in language. It speaks in rhythm. In pattern. In repetition. You do not have to fight your old habits. You only have to replace them with better ones and repeat. You are not stuck. You are simply conditioned. And what has been conditioned can be reconditioned. So begin today with one choice. Not a perfect one, just a conscious one. And let your future self thank you for rehearsing the right story.

Clarity Before Action

"Having clear vision is a personal blessing."

What if taking action too soon is what's keeping you stuck?

We live in a culture obsessed with movement. Do more. Be busy. Hustle. Take massive action. From every corner of the self-help world, we are told that success favours the bold, that the path will become clear once you start walking. And while there is some truth to that, it also ignores a quieter reality, one often overlooked – that action without clarity is not progress, it is noise. Worse, it is a distraction dressed up as discipline.

This chapter is about what happens when you learn to pause, not out of fear but out of wisdom. It's about the power of waiting until your inner landscape aligns with your outer moves, because when you act before you're clear, you end up building a life that doesn't fit you. And then you call it fate.

After my second divorce, I felt an overwhelming need to do something, anything, to fix it all, to rebuild, to prove that I was not broken. I cleaned the house obsessively, took on more work, said yes to things that didn't align. On the outside, I looked functional. On the inside, I was a whirlwind. I was moving, but not forward – just fast. Then one night, in the stillness of an ordinary Tuesday, I sat outside with nothing but a cup of tea. I looked up at the stars and asked a question that changed everything: what if doing more right now is actually hurting me?

It was confronting, because I had always measured my worth by what I did, not by what I understood. And in that silence, I began to see it. I wasn't acting from vision. I was acting from panic. Brian Tracy teaches something that few people absorb the first time they hear it: "Clarity is the starting point of all success." Not effort. Not action. Clarity. You cannot hit a target you can't see, and you cannot see clearly if you are always in motion. We've been conditioned to confuse activity with purpose, but clarity doesn't come from noise. It comes from stillness. It arrives in those moments when you aren't trying to force it, when your mind is not chasing a dozen unfinished tasks, when your subconscious is finally free to speak. And it does speak – not in chaos, but in calm.

Dr. Joe Dispenza reveals that when we act from stress, we are not truly creating. We are surviving. We repeat old patterns, old beliefs, old chemistry. Stress narrows our vision. We don't innovate – we react. Think about the last time you rushed into a decision because you felt you had to. How much of that choice came from a calm, centred place? For most people, the answer is none. I've made career moves, said yes to relationships, poured money into projects – all without clarity. Each time, it felt like progress, but in hindsight, it was just movement without meaning. What I really needed was permission to pause.

One of the subconscious mind's greatest roles is filtration. It takes in everything – all sights, sounds, thoughts, ideas – and then organises it based on what you've trained it to value. But if you never give it time to process, it becomes clogged. You begin responding to life through a clouded lens – emotionally fogged, mentally cluttered, spiritually tired. Silence is what clears the lens. Clarity is what emerges when the noise dies down. And from that clarity, action becomes obvious – not forced.

In Sacred Stones, I explore the symbolism of stone stacking – how each rock must be chosen with intention, with weight, with balance. It is an act of presence, and it mirrors life. When we stack decisions without clarity, the entire structure becomes unstable. But when we place each with calm awareness, the result is something sacred, something lasting.

It wasn't easy at first. My instincts wanted to act, to fix, to move. But I trained myself to pause. To ask before acting: is this coming from peace or panic? Do I know the why behind this choice? If I wait one more day, would that change how I feel? Over time, I noticed a shift. I became slower, but sharper. I made fewer moves, but better ones. People noticed. They would ask, how are you so calm when everything is so uncertain? And the answer was always the same: because I stopped rushing clarity.

Cal Newport dismantles the myth of immediate response. He reminds us that urgency is often manufactured – by systems, expectations, and insecurity. But meaningful work, meaningful living, requires space. Breathing room. Thoughtfulness. The subconscious thrives in that space. Not when it is rushed. But when it is trusted.

We are told to take action. But the truth is, sometimes the most powerful action is no action – yet. Sometimes the most profound move is the decision to wait, to listen, to become clear. You are not falling behind if you pause. You are setting the foundation for a life that actually fits.

So before you build, listen. Before you act, align. Before you leap, look inward. Because when clarity leads – everything that follows begins to feel like truth.

Quiet Confidence

"Being content and confident is a personal blessing."

What if the loudest person in the room is the most unsure, and your calm is your greatest power?

Confidence is too often misunderstood. In today's world, it has become loud, performative, and easily mistaken for charisma. We associate it with those who speak up in meetings, dominate discussions, take centre stage and collect applause. But real confidence does not draw attention to itself. It doesn't need to. It is content to exist in silence. It does not seek permission, validation, or a crowd.

I used to think I had to be louder to be seen. At work, at home, even in my internal dialogue, I equated volume with strength. I spoke quickly, took charge, asserted opinions. I confused control with confidence, and I believed that to lead, I had to overpower. But what I was actually doing was masking my insecurity with noise. I needed people to agree with me to feel safe. I needed control to feel stable. I needed the last word so I wouldn't feel irrelevant. Underneath it all was a desperate longing to be heard, because deep down I was afraid I didn't matter.

Then something shifted. I discovered silence, and with it came the realisation that power didn't come from being louder - it came from listening. Not just to others, but to myself. As I spent more time alone after my second divorce, without the usual distractions or demands of others' expectations, I slowly began to hear my own voice. Not the reactive one, shaped by fear or habit, but the deeper, truer one underneath it all. And I found I could trust it.

Cal Newport teaches that deep work builds deep confidence. He explains that when you engage in focused, meaningful work in solitude, you create internal evidence of your capability. You no longer need others to tell you that you're good enough. You know it, because you've watched yourself rise to challenges, again and again, when no one was watching. That's the essence of quiet confidence. It's not about looking strong. It's about being stable.

Silence became my teacher. I remember a specific moment at work when I was unfairly accused of something. The old me would have jumped to defend myself, eager to fix the misunderstanding and clear my name. But instead, I paused. I chose silence first. I took a breath, then responded with calm clarity. I didn't rush. I didn't react. I simply stood in my truth. And something changed in the room. I wasn't walked over. I was respected. That was the day I realised I no longer needed to win the room. I only needed to hold my ground.

Stillness gave me that. It trained me to value presence over persuasion, integrity over image, and depth over dominance.

In Phobia Fighter, I wrote about how fear often disguises itself as control. When we're afraid, we try to manage everything - people, outcomes, impressions. We rush to speak, to act, to prove ourselves. But silence taught me that real strength lies in restraint. When you've made peace with your fear, you no longer need to react from it. You can sit in discomfort without letting it steer your choices. You can listen to others without needing to correct them. You can walk away from conflict without feeling diminished.

Dr. Joe Dispenza shares that the subconscious mind mirrors the state of your nervous system. When your body is calm, your mind receives the message that you are safe. Over time, that message becomes your new baseline. You stop performing. You stop compensating. You start trusting. And that trust shows up in the smallest moments - when you let someone be wrong without fixing it, when you speak with less urgency, when you no longer feel the need to be right to feel worthy.

The evolution was slow but steady. As I embraced silence more consistently, I began to notice a difference in how I carried myself. I no longer needed to posture. I could sit in a room and speak only when I had something meaningful to say. I could leave things unresolved without spiralling into anxiety. I could say, "I'm not sure," and not feel ashamed. That was new for me. That was powerful.

Brian Tracy says that confidence comes from competence, and competence comes from repetition. But he also points out that confidence grows even faster when we act in alignment with our values. That stuck with me. As I made silence a regular practice and focused more on what mattered - integrity, growth, peace - I began to like the man I was becoming. And when you genuinely like yourself, you no longer need the applause of others.

You become anchored.

Confidence becomes less about being seen and more about being steady. You stop looking outward for approval and start looking inward for alignment. You speak less, but your words carry more weight. You listen more, but you aren't absorbing other people's insecurities. You stop reacting. You start responding. You walk through life not to impress, but to express - to live in a way that reflects who you are when no one is watching.

I used to fill space with noise. Now I honour space with silence. I used to need the last word. Now I value the last thought. I used to seek power in presence. Now I find power in peace.

There is a version of confidence that doesn't need to announce itself. It lives in the quiet choices, in the unspoken truths, in the decisions no one else sees. It lives in the man who walks away from drama, the woman who doesn't need to explain herself, the child who knows their worth without comparison. It lives in you - when you allow silence to shape you.

In the end, confidence is not loud. It does not shout over others. It does not wear a mask. It is the sound of your soul breathing freely. It is the way your body relaxes when you know you have nothing to prove. It is the permission you give yourself to be enough, as you are.

So sit still. Let your silence do the talking. Let your presence be your proof.

That is quiet confidence - and no one can take it from you.

Mental Boundaries

What if your mind feels heavy not because of what is in it, but because you never learned how to protect it?

There comes a point in healing when the problem is no longer what happened to you, but what you continue to allow into your mind. We spend so much time trying to fix, forgive or forget, yet rarely do we pause to ask whether we've built the internal walls necessary to prevent the same damage from entering again. Mental boundaries are not merely about saying no to others, they are about saying yes to your peace. They are not about creating distance from people, but about carving space for clarity. They are not harsh, nor cold, nor rude - they are sacred.

If silence is the doorway to the subconscious, then boundaries are the lock. Without them, you are constantly exposed, inviting in every opinion, fear, criticism and comparison, then wondering why your thoughts are muddled and your heart feels heavy. Before I understood boundaries, my mind was like an open window in a storm. I absorbed the moods of others, their opinions, their projections. I felt responsible for how people saw me. I explained myself too much, justified my choices, tiptoed around reactions that weren't mine to manage - and all of it was exhausting.

In the wake of my second divorce, this became more acute. My mind often felt like a crowded room, full of voices but very few of them were mine. Judgement, regret, blame and shame echoed louder than any sense of self. I remember realising, with a jolt of clarity one night, that I had no filter. Everything came in. Nothing was sorted or sifted. I had become mentally porous - and it was draining me.

That evening, instead of my usual rituals, I simply sat outside. No television, no phone, not even a glass of wine. Just the fading light, the sky overhead, and the silence I had long forgotten how to sit in. For the first time in a long while, I noticed a tightness in my chest that had been there for months, maybe years. And I finally asked myself - what was I holding? Old arguments, work stress, a friend's offhand comment, fragments of social media noise, guilt, worry, the "should haves" and the "what ifs." None of it belonged to me, yet I had made space for all of it.

That night marked the turning point. I didn't need more opinions, more conversations or more information. I needed boundaries. Psychological, emotional, even spiritual. A filter for what I would let in and what I would gently close the door on.

Dr. Joe Dispenza writes that the thoughts we think most frequently become our internal programming. Repetition creates identity. So when we live on high alert, when we rehearse guilt or defensiveness or self-doubt, our subconscious assumes that is who we are. He teaches that energy flows where attention goes - and without mental boundaries, our attention is hijacked by others, by the past, by media, by our own unexamined conditioning. If you don't protect your mental space, someone else will fill it - with their version of your reality.

Boundaries, then, are not barriers to love or connection. They are filters for alignment. They help you decide what deserves your energy, which thoughts are worthy of your inner sanctuary, which voices are valuable, and which should fade into the background.

They are how you teach your subconscious what matters. Because the subconscious does not judge or critique - it adapts. If you allow chaos and noise to dominate your thinking, your subconscious will normalise it and rewire you accordingly. If you cultivate peace and clarity, it will begin building your identity around those frequencies instead.

In Shadow Work Evolution, I unpack this further. Poor boundaries often originate from childhood conditioning - being told to be agreeable, avoid conflict, earn love through self-sacrifice. You become accustomed to swallowing your truth, apologising for having needs, feeling guilty for taking up space. Over time, your sense of self becomes shaped by what others expect, not by what you truly believe. The shadow of people pleasing is deep, but once you shine light on it, you find something unexpected beneath - freedom.

I remember the first time I said no, not out of anger, but from a place of self-respect. A colleague began venting to me for the third time that week about an issue that didn't involve me. Normally I would have listened, absorbed, nodded. But this time I said calmly, "I'm not available to carry that today." It was awkward. He blinked, surprised. I smiled gently. And the moment passed. But something shifted inside me. I had chosen peace. I had drawn a quiet line. And nothing fell apart.

That is when I began to understand - boundaries are not just statements. They are spiritual acts. They are how you remind yourself that you matter, that your time and energy are not public property. They are how you reclaim your inner space.

Brian Tracy says that clarity and focus go hand in hand. He advises us to regularly review what we allow into our lives - from conversations and habits to the information we consume.

Boundaries support that clarity. They act as mental gatekeepers, protecting your energy so that your efforts are aligned, your focus is sharp and your sense of purpose remains undisturbed.

This is where Eulogy Writing unexpectedly connects. That book taught me to see life through the lens of legacy. When we write eulogies, the noise fades. We don't remember the gossip, the drama or the distractions. We remember the essence - kindness, courage, quiet presence. Boundaries, then, are your way of living now with the same intentionality you hope to be remembered for later. They strip away the unnecessary and return you to what truly matters.

As I practised silence more deeply and became consistent in my boundaries, I noticed real changes. I no longer engaged in gossip. I spent less time with those who drained my energy. I curated my news intake and social media consumption. I allowed people to misunderstand me without feeling the need to correct them. Each of these choices became a message to my subconscious: "We are safe. We are centred. We choose what enters."

And the response? My mind felt clearer. My thoughts became slower, more deliberate. My creativity returned with more ease. I started to feel like the driver of my life again, not the passenger. The noise receded. The clarity grew.

Your subconscious watches what you tolerate. If you tolerate chaos, it assumes that is your baseline. If you accept disrespect, it learns to dim your self-worth. But if you set boundaries, protect your peace and make space for stillness, it responds with calm and clarity. The subconscious is always listening - and learning.

Boundaries teach it that you value yourself, that you are not available for everything, that you are not required to respond to every provocation, nor participate in every emotional loop. You are allowed to be selective. You are allowed to be quiet. You are allowed to protect your mind.

There is something sacred about a well-guarded inner world. It becomes a sanctuary, not a battlefield. A place of strength, not survival. When you build boundaries from the inside out, they no longer feel like fences - they feel like freedom. They become not walls, but invitations - to peace, to self-respect, to inner strength. They remind you, and everyone around you, that your mind is not a dumping ground. It is sacred ground. And it deserves to be protected.

Let that be your new normal.

Part III: Living in Alignment

Peaceful Productivity

"Being energetic and diligent is a personal blessing."

What if the key to achieving more isn't doing more, but needing less?

We were never meant to be machines, yet somehow, we've built lives that worship output. We celebrate the early riser, glorify the hustle, and revere the person who seems to juggle everything at once. "I'm so busy" has become a badge of honour, worn with pride, even as it drains us. But what happens when the very thing we chase - productivity - becomes the thief of our peace?

Peaceful productivity may sound like a contradiction, yet it is the most natural state of flow we can experience. It does not mean doing less, nor does it suggest a lack of ambition. It means shifting from force to flow, from panic to presence, and from measuring success by quantity to honouring it through clarity and alignment. It is a quiet but powerful rebellion against a culture that equates worth with busyness.

There was a time when I believed productivity had to hurt. I was juggling teaching, single fatherhood, emotional recovery, and the thousand small tasks that make up adult life. Every day began in a rush and ended in depletion. I saw exhaustion as a sign that I had done enough. Rest was something to be earned - after everything and everyone else had been taken care of. I collapsed into bed not satisfied, but spent. I wasn't building a life - I was surviving one.

The shift began when I came across Brian Tracy's principle that "every minute spent in planning saves ten in execution." At first glance, it felt like another time management slogan, but in practice, it opened something deeper. I started my mornings differently, not with the glow of screens or the mental noise of tasks waiting to be done, but with silence. I took a walk. I brewed tea and drank it slowly. I read one short reflection from 365 Days of SOUL. I let my thoughts settle before deciding anything.

Then I asked myself one simple question: What is essential today?

That question cut through the clutter. I realised that most of what filled my calendar wasn't necessary - it was inherited. Assumed. Unquestioned. By letting my subconscious speak before the world shouted at me, I gained clarity, not just about what to do, but how to be while doing it.

In 365 Days of SOUL, the rhythm of short, reflective entries became a gentle guide, nudging me away from urgency and towards alignment. Each day's message reminded me that doing can come from stillness, that action doesn't need to be chaotic to be effective, and that some of our most impactful choices begin in silence.

Dr. Joe Dispenza's work confirmed what I was beginning to live - that when we operate from stress, our minds are in survival mode. In this state, the subconscious mind becomes reactive, constantly scanning for threats, stuck in cycles of fight or flight. We lose the ability to create, to imagine, to build with intent. By contrast, when the mind is calm, the body feels safe, and the subconscious becomes a tool of insight and flow rather than defence.

This understanding shifted my view of discipline. I used to think discipline meant pushing harder, staying up later, saying yes more often. But now, discipline looked like protecting my time, turning down distractions, knowing when to pause, and, most importantly, trusting that my worth wasn't tied to my output.

Cal Newport calls this shift from reactive to intentional "deep work" - focused, uninterrupted time dedicated to meaningful efforts. I began structuring my days around blocks of deep work. No notifications, no switching tabs, no multitasking. Just me, my thoughts, and the task at hand. Whether it was writing a chapter or planning a new project, I immersed myself fully, and as a result, my work became lighter, faster, and far more enjoyable.

Peaceful productivity, I discovered, is less about effort and more about elimination. It's about removing what dilutes your focus, drains your energy, or clouds your purpose. I stopped filling every gap in my day. I said no more often. I made peace with unfinished lists, knowing that most of what felt urgent wasn't actually important.

The more I practised this, the more I noticed something powerful: I was getting more done, not by working harder, but by working clearer. And I liked myself more while doing it.

The guilt I once felt for resting faded as I witnessed the quality of my output improve. I began to trust that silence wasn't lazy, it was strategic. That space wasn't empty, it was sacred. That slowing down didn't mean falling behind - it meant catching up with my soul.

Brian Tracy reminds us that clarity and focus go hand in hand. His suggestion to regularly audit your commitments helped me see that I had been carrying things out of habit, not intention. I started each week with reflection, not rush. I stopped measuring success by how many emails I sent, and started measuring it by how I felt at the end of the day. Did I feel proud? Grounded? In flow?

One of the most surprising tools in my shift to peaceful productivity was Sacred Stones. A book born from silence itself, it explores the symbolism of balance and presence. Stacking stones became a metaphor for my new approach: deliberate, centred, intentional. No stone placed in haste. Every one chosen with care.

The productivity I know now feels like alignment. It isn't loud. It doesn't seek applause. It doesn't demand perfection. It feels like knowing what matters, doing just that, and letting go of the rest. It feels like starting the day with clarity, moving through it with focus, and ending it with peace - not regret or fatigue.

It's taken years to unlearn the lie that worth is earned through depletion. Now, I believe worth is recognised in the quiet, in how we protect our energy, in how we serve our purpose without burning out. Peaceful productivity is not a system - it is a mindset. One that honours your time, your soul, and your sanity.

So here's the truth I leave with you: Productivity without peace is performance. Productivity with peace is power.

Choose wisely.

Authentic Alignment

"Living a life of integrity brings true joy."

What if the real burnout you feel isn't from overwork, but from living a life that doesn't match who you really are?

We are taught to strive, to hustle, to achieve. But what if all that striving has been slowly pulling you away from yourself? What if the fatigue is not from the load, but from the misalignment?

There comes a moment in almost every person's life when the external mask begins to feel heavier than the face beneath it. You may have felt this already – that subtle, gnawing discontent that no amount of success can quiet. A quiet discomfort that creeps in when you're doing everything you were told would bring happiness, and yet, you feel strangely disconnected from the life you're living.

That is the soul's way of asking you to realign.

For me, the moment of reckoning came not with a bang, but with a silence so deep it startled me. I remember coming home after a long day of teaching, dropping my bag by the door, and staring blankly into the quiet. No noise, no distractions, just a stillness that mirrored how lost I felt inside. I had spent years moving from goal to goal, performing roles I never questioned. Teacher. Husband. Father. Colleague. Provider. But somewhere along the way, I had stopped asking one of the most important questions – does this reflect who I truly am?

Authentic alignment isn't about abandoning responsibilities or tearing down everything you've built. It's about meeting yourself again – with honesty, without the pressure to impress, and with a deep curiosity about what truly feels right, not just what looks right.

Dr Joe Dispenza explains that the body is the unconscious mind. It memorises emotions, routines, and even identities, until your life becomes an expression of the past rather than a conscious creation of the present. This is why change can feel so threatening. You are not just trying to shift a habit, but to rewrite a deeply ingrained identity that has kept you safe, or at least familiar, for years.

When I began to listen to that inner dissonance, I didn't yet have words for it. I only knew that certain things drained me, while others quietly lit me up. The difference wasn't in their difficulty, but in their resonance. I could lead a parent meeting and feel flat, but spend half an hour writing or walking in silence and feel mysteriously energised. It was a strange sensation, as if my subconscious was gently tugging me toward something truer, something quieter, something more alive.

This was not about escape. It was about return.

I began small. A decision here, a no where I used to say yes, a pause where I used to push through. I started watching my reactions more closely – not to judge them, but to understand them. I paid attention to where my body tightened, where my spirit contracted, and where, instead, I felt open, peaceful, and connected.

Brian Tracy writes that "peace of mind is the highest human good." But that peace cannot exist without integrity. And integrity isn't just about ethics – it's about wholeness. It's about living in such a way that your actions, your values, and your inner knowing all speak the same language.

For years, my actions were louder than my awareness. I was praised for being efficient, reliable, always available. But that availability came at the cost of my own needs. My silence became the space where I began to tell the truth. I stopped pretending to enjoy things I didn't. I gave up the exhausting habit of apologising for my boundaries. I started honouring the parts of me I had ignored in favour of being liked.

And in that honouring, I found something I had not felt in years – joy. Not the kind that comes from achievements, but the quieter, deeper kind that lives in the knowledge that you are living your truth, even when no one is watching.

Cal Newport's insights on deep work go far beyond productivity. He suggests that depth itself is a form of alignment – that to do anything with genuine presence, we must be congruent in our values and our environment. When we are scattered, when we say yes to what doesn't serve us, we break that internal coherence. And without coherence, we lose the ability to focus, to create, and to live with meaning.

I had spent decades being fragmented, offering parts of myself to everyone else. But wholeness, I began to see, was not about giving everything to everyone. It was about choosing what parts of myself I wanted to strengthen, and letting go of the versions of me that were simply surviving.

In my book Shadow Work Evolution, I explore how masks are formed – not from malice, but from adaptation. As children, we learn quickly which behaviours bring acceptance and which ones invite rejection. We internalise the idea that authenticity is risky. So we create personas. We please. We achieve. We perform. But in doing so, we quietly exile the truest parts of ourselves.

Reclaiming those parts takes courage. But the cost of not doing so is far greater.

When you live out of alignment for too long, your body keeps score. Fatigue, resentment, anxiety, and numbness are often not signs of a weak mind, but of a misaligned life. Your subconscious knows when your actions betray your inner truth, even if your conscious mind hasn't caught up yet.

The blessing that accompanies authentic alignment is quiet but profound – you begin to feel at home in yourself again.

You no longer need to over-explain. You no longer seek constant reassurance. You stop measuring your worth through comparison. You begin to trust that what is meant for you will resonate, not require performance.

There were moments in my transition toward alignment that were incredibly lonely. Not because I was physically alone, but because I had to let go of roles and relationships that were built on an inauthentic version of me. But what I gained in return was priceless – the ability to look at myself in the mirror and feel a quiet pride in who I was becoming.

Authenticity is not something you arrive at. It is something you practise. Each day offers small invitations to return to yourself. A choice to be honest. A moment to pause before reacting. A decision to rest instead of push. These are not dramatic gestures. They are simple acts of remembrance.

    i.   You remember what you love.
    ii. You remember what you need.
    iii. You remember who you were before the world told you who to be.

And slowly, your life begins to reshape itself around that truth.

Authentic alignment is not about having all the answers. It is about asking better questions. It is about listening for the still voice beneath the noise and daring to respond, even when it asks you to walk a quieter, less travelled path.

i. You do not need to perform to be loved.
ii. You do not need to be perfect to be worthy.
iii. You do not need to be understood to be true.
iv. You only need to be honest.

And when you are, your subconscious responds. It stops trying to protect you from being yourself. It starts partnering with you, showing you the next right step, not from fear, but from resonance.

So if something in your life feels off, do not rush to fix it. Sit with it. Listen. Let the silence show you where the misalignment lives. Then, step by step, realign. Not to please others, but to honour the truth that lives in you.

Because that truth – unfiltered, unforced, and fully lived – is where the joy begins.

That is authentic alignment.

The Illusion of Control

"Letting go of attachment is a supreme blessing."

What if the thing you're holding onto the tightest is the very thing keeping you stuck?

We have been taught that control is strength. That holding on tightly, planning obsessively, and micromanaging outcomes is what keeps us safe. From childhood, we are encouraged to steer the wheel, to take charge, to fight chaos with order. But few of us are told the cost of this illusion. Control, for all its posturing, often masks a deeper truth: fear.

The fear of being hurt again. The fear of the unknown. The fear of failure, rejection, humiliation, or grief. Beneath control is the aching need to protect ourselves from an inner world we cannot fully predict, and an outer world that offers no guarantees. Yet ironically, it is this very need to control that fractures our peace. The subconscious, ever watchful, interprets chronic control as a message: the world is unsafe, and I am not enough to handle it as it is.

I began to see the illusion of control not during a dramatic life event, but in the small moments - an ordinary conversation with my adult son, a morning routine thrown off by a missed alarm, a technology hiccup that left me spiralling with frustration. These were not catastrophes, yet I watched myself react as if they were threats. My breath would shorten, my mind would race to fix what wasn't broken, my words would sharpen, and my shoulders would tighten with an invisible burden I had carried most of my life - the burden of trying to keep everything from falling apart.

But it wasn't everything I was trying to manage. It was me. The illusion of control is really the subconscious gripping at old wounds. It's a child within who once experienced unpredictability and vowed never to feel that powerless again. And so we create systems, routines, rigid expectations, and labels to avoid the discomfort of surrender.

Dr Joe Dispenza speaks often of the neurological patterning that happens when we relive emotional memories through thoughts. The body becomes addicted to the hormones of stress, anxiety, and vigilance. We begin each day rehearsing danger, preparing for the worst, planning not out of passion, but out of fear. The subconscious, flooded with stress signals, cannot rest. It cannot imagine a better future because it is stuck defending a past it believes will repeat. And so we live in survival, mistaking it for responsibility.

When I truly understood this, it shifted everything. I had always prided myself on being responsible. A father. A teacher. A provider. I planned holidays with precision, budgets with military discipline, and even conversations with my spouse like mental scripts I practised in advance. I thought this made me wise, careful, maybe even admirable. But in truth, it made me rigid. And deeply afraid of spontaneity. Because spontaneity, to the subconscious obsessed with control, feels like danger.

I remember the moment the truth cracked open. I was in the garden one Saturday morning, tending to the same patch of herbs I had grown for years. The coriander was dying, as it always did mid-season, despite my best efforts. I knelt in the dirt, digging and pruning, caught in my usual silent frustration. I had done everything right. Why was it still wilting?

And then it hit me: I had not accepted the cycle of the plant. I had tried to out-control nature. And in that moment, I saw it everywhere - I was not nurturing life, I was managing it. I wasn't responding to what was, I was fighting what I believed should be. Control had stolen my ability to trust that life has its own intelligence, and that intelligence speaks when we stop gripping.

Brian Tracy offers a powerful distinction between responsibility and control. Responsibility, he says, is the ability to respond. It is an empowered posture. Control, on the other hand, is fear disguised as authority. It creates resistance. It blocks flow. And it feeds the subconscious a dangerous message: I do not trust life, so I must force it to bend to my will.

It was only through sustained silence that I began to rewire this. I practised letting go in ways that felt unnatural. I delayed decisions. I allowed others to speak without rushing to fill the space. I stopped rehearsing conversations in my head. I walked without tracking my steps. I wrote without knowing the ending. I sat in the unknown without needing it to resolve.

At first, it was agonising. Every part of me wanted to reach for structure. I felt the itch to fix, to steer, to know. But I stayed. And slowly, something strange happened - I began to feel safe. Not because anything outside of me had changed. But because I had changed my relationship with the unknown. I stopped demanding certainty, and started inviting trust.

This shift is not something that can be taught in a seminar. It is felt in the body, in the nervous system, in the softening of breath and shoulders and tongue. It is not theoretical. It is cellular.

Cal Newport speaks of the value of structure not as a prison, but as a frame for freedom. True structure is not about control. It is about rhythm. Rhythm creates space for depth. And depth requires trust. Trust that you do not need to monitor every detail. Trust that your subconscious knows how to solve problems without panic. Trust that your soul knows how to find peace without perfect answers.

In my book Shadow Work Evolution, I explore how control is often a learned response from emotional pain. We grow up in environments where love was conditional, affection was unpredictable, or boundaries were violated. And so we internalise the belief: if I can control everything, I won't get hurt. But this belief becomes a cage. It keeps us small, reactive, and disconnected from the flow of life that is always trying to move us towards wholeness.

Letting go of control is not giving up. It is opening up. It is the radical act of allowing your life to unfold in a way that may be better than you planned. It is trusting that your intuition, your subconscious, and your connection to something higher will not abandon you. It is returning to the body when the mind wants to race. It is breathing through the unknown rather than bargaining with it. And it is learning to live in alignment, not manipulation.

The most peaceful people I know are not those with perfect routines. They are the ones who have learned to meet life as it comes, with open palms and softened hearts. They still plan. But they are not bound to those plans. They still care. But they are not controlled by outcomes. They still feel. But they are not consumed by fear.

This is not a one-time choice. It is a daily practice. Every moment of anxiety is an invitation to soften. Every moment of frustration is a chance to loosen the grip. Every time we feel the urge to control, we are being shown where we are afraid to trust. And that trust begins not in the external world, but in the quiet within.

You may be walking through something right now that feels uncertain. A relationship. A diagnosis. A financial stretch. A spiritual void. Your first instinct will be to tighten. To manage. To micromanage. But let this be your invitation to do something different. To breathe. To listen. To loosen. And to trust that even in this, especially in this, you are being guided.

Let go. Not in defeat, but in devotion. Not in apathy, but in alignment. Let go so that something wiser can enter. Let go so that your subconscious can show you what it knows. Let go so that your nervous system can remember what peace feels like.

The illusion of control will always tempt you back. But once you have tasted the stillness on the other side of surrender, you will never confuse fear for power again.

And that, perhaps, is the greatest blessing of all.

Aligned Living

"Living in harmony with truth brings supreme blessings."

What if the unease you feel is not a failure of mindset, but a quiet rebellion from your soul, begging you to live a life that fits?

We talk about alignment as if it is a spiritual luxury, a reward for those who meditate enough, journal often, or practise yoga at sunrise. But alignment is not decorative. It is foundational. It is the deep current that carries your life in the right direction, whether or not the surface is still.

The trouble is, most people are not living in alignment. They are living in roles. They wear the suit of responsibility, the mask of confidence, the script of social acceptance. They meet expectations they never set, chase goals they do not value, and speak words that feel foreign the moment they leave their lips. Then they wonder why anxiety lingers like a fog, why burnout arrives uninvited, why life, even when full, feels hollow.

Living in alignment means living in agreement with your own truth. It means your actions echo your values. Your choices reflect your clarity. Your no has as much integrity as your yes. And most of all, it means that the person you are when nobody is watching is the same person who walks into the room. There is no costume to remove. No mask to adjust. Just congruence.

When I first stumbled into this idea, it was not in a workshop or a self-help book. It was in the middle of a breakdown. I was saying yes to too many things, managing too many impressions, spreading myself thinner and thinner. And in the silence of a late Sunday evening, I looked at my own reflection and whispered, I do not recognise this man. Not because I was lost, but because I had been wearing too many layers of someone I thought I was supposed to be.

Brian Tracy speaks to this with clarity. He teaches that integrity is the foundation of lasting confidence, and that peace of mind comes when your outer world aligns with your inner principles. The moment I heard that, I stopped what I was doing. Because I had been aiming for success, but not checking if it matched my internal compass. I had been building momentum, but not direction.

Alignment is not found in doing more. It is found in doing what matters. And often, that means doing less. Saying no to good things so you can say yes to the right things. It is not always dramatic. Sometimes it looks like declining a dinner that feels performative. Sometimes it is letting go of a business opportunity that pays well but costs your soul. Sometimes it is as simple as changing your morning routine to match your actual energy rather than someone else's blueprint.

Dr. Joe Dispenza says that your thoughts create your reality, but more importantly, the feeling behind your thoughts becomes the signal you send to the universe. If you are doing all the "right" things but feeling resentment, fatigue or misalignment, then that frequency speaks louder than your goals. The subconscious does not obey language. It obeys energy. And if your energy is out of alignment with your actions, your results will be skewed. They might look good on paper but feel empty in your chest.

I learned this the slow way. I said yes to writing projects that felt hollow. I overcommitted in areas that looked impressive but left me drained. And worst of all, I ignored the whisper that said, This

66

is not your work. The whisper grew louder, not in words, but in physical signals. I began to feel tight in my chest when I opened certain emails. I felt heavy walking into meetings that once excited me. My sleep fractured. My moods became unpredictable. And still, I told myself I was just tired.

But the truth was, I was misaligned.

Alignment is physical. It is emotional. It is spiritual. And your body knows before your mind will admit it. I had to go quiet enough to hear it. I had to stop listening to my own justifications and start listening to the subtle cues that had been trying to guide me all along.

Suggested Companion Title: Shadow Work Evolution. In this book, I explored what it means to live in truth when the ego wants control. Shadow work taught me that misalignment is often a protective layer we construct to avoid the pain of being vulnerable. But in peeling back those layers, in facing the discomfort, we begin to remember who we were before we started performing. That raw, unedited self is where alignment begins.

Cal Newport offers something deeply practical in this conversation. He says that true focus is not just about blocking distractions, but about creating a life that is centred on what really matters. He speaks of "lifestyle-centred career planning," which means you design your professional life around your values, not the other way round. That idea stayed with me. I realised that I was asking life to support my work, rather than building work that supported my life.

So I made a change. It started with one question, asked daily in the quiet hours before the world wakes up: What feels true today?

Some days the answer was rest. Some days it was writing. Some days it was sitting with a friend in need, without needing to fix them. But each day I followed that truth, I felt stronger. Lighter. Clearer. More like the man I had almost forgotten I could be.

I stopped splitting myself between versions. I stopped trying to be everything to everyone. I became deeply selective with how I spent my time, who I allowed into my sacred space, and what I gave my energy to. This wasn't selfish. It was necessary.

When you live in alignment, decisions become easier. You do not need to ask a dozen people what you should do. You know. You feel it. It sits in your bones like a quiet yes or a clear no. You don't explain your boundaries. You live them. You don't chase people who don't get you. You bless their path and stay on your own. You don't apologise for your joy or shrink for someone else's comfort.

And when misalignment appears, you catch it quickly. You notice the way your body tenses. You observe the way your voice changes when you speak a half-truth. You become sensitive to your own disconnection. And rather than judge it, you correct it.

That is what living aligned looks like. It is not a performance. It is not a brand. It is a conversation between your soul and your schedule.

There was a time when I measured success by external milestones. Now, I measure it by peace. If my peace is intact, if my energy is clean, if my inner voice feels heard and honoured, then I am aligned. And alignment has a beautiful way of attracting what is meant for you without force.

I remember walking away from a partnership that looked promising on paper. Every logical part of me said to stay. But something deeper said, This is not your path. I chose silence. I waited. I said no. And within weeks, a different door opened - one that matched not just my skills, but my soul. That is the grace of alignment. It makes room for what fits when you release what doesn't.

This journey is not about perfection. I still get pulled. I still forget. But the difference is, I come back faster. I come back without shame. And I come back to a self I actually enjoy being.

Alignment, in the end, is not a destination. It is a way of walking. A way of being. A daily decision to honour what is true, even when it is inconvenient.

If you feel restless, if you feel unfulfilled despite doing all the "right" things, pause. Breathe. Ask: Where am I saying yes out of fear, and no to what brings me alive?

This is your invitation.

Live from the inside out. Trust your timing. Trust your values. Trust that the quieter path is often the truest. And when you feel the deep hum of peace beneath your choices, you will know: this is alignment.

This is you, returned to yourself.

Magnetic Mindset

"Guarding the mind with right thoughts brings blessing."

What if every belief you hold is either attracting your future or repelling it?

This is not about magic. This is about the invisible architecture of your life, quietly designed by your thoughts, repeated every day until they become your identity. You cannot think small and live large. You cannot rehearse lack and manifest abundance. You cannot entertain doubt and expect confidence to grow.

Your mindset is not a mood. It is a magnet. And it is always working, whether you're paying attention or not.

This is what I began to realise during the deeper stages of my silence. When the outer noise had faded, I became aware of a subtler noise, an inner dialogue so constant it had almost become invisible. A running commentary beneath my choices. It said things like, That's not for you. You'll be judged. Don't try that, you'll look foolish. Stay safe, stay quiet, stay hidden. These weren't dramatic thoughts. They were habitual. Low-level. And deeply magnetic. Because even when I acted confidently, those beliefs tugged on the reins behind me.

Dr. Joe Dispenza teaches that "your personality creates your personal reality." And personality, he explains, is a product of how you think, act, and feel every single day. If you do not change your internal state, you keep reproducing the same external circumstances. It is not a punishment. It's a loop. The subconscious does not change because you wish it to. It changes when you break the pattern.

For years, I had unknowingly rehearsed a mindset shaped by fear. Not dramatic fear, but subtle limitations. I called it "being realistic." I told myself I was staying grounded, being responsible. But in truth, I was reinforcing beliefs that had expired. Beliefs inherited from teachers, parents, religion, failed relationships, cultural conditioning. I had never questioned them, only lived them.

Brian Tracy confirms this trap. He says, "You begin to fly when you let go of self-limiting beliefs and allow your mind and aspirations to rise to greater heights." It sounds obvious. But few people actually take inventory of their beliefs. Fewer still challenge them. Most of us live in inherited thoughts. Second-hand stories. Emotional hand-me-downs passed off as truth.

It wasn't until I consciously started replacing my internal vocabulary that things began to shift. I stopped saying, "I can't." I replaced it with, "How can I?" I stopped thinking, "That's not me." I replaced it with, "Who says?" I began to question the finality of my own thoughts. And in that questioning, I found power.

A magnetic mindset is not blind optimism. It is disciplined focus. It is the decision to train your mind towards your vision, not your history. To take hold of your subconscious patterns and speak to them with clarity. You don't just believe in possibility. You practise it.

This was where the power of visualisation became a daily tool. I would sit in stillness and not just imagine success, but feel it. What does alignment feel like in the body? What does freedom taste like in the moment? What would confidence do in this situation? I wasn't just thinking differently. I was rehearsing a new emotional state. And the subconscious began to respond. Because it doesn't know the difference between real and imagined. It only knows repetition.

Suggested Companion Title: 365 Days of SOUL

This book series was my personal practice in mindset shift. Each daily entry was a mirror. Not just a motivational phrase, but an invitation to feel something higher, to think something deeper, to rehearse a better inner world. Readers who stayed with it discovered the same thing I did: a magnetic mindset is built one thought at a time.

Cal Newport talks about intentionality as the defining feature of success in a distracted world. In his framework, deep focus is how we break free from default behaviours. This applies not only to tasks, but to thinking itself. Most people are not thinking. They are reacting. They are rerunning a script written long ago. But when you stop reacting and begin thinking on purpose, you disrupt the loop.

That's what I did. I became a disruptor of my own mind.

When I would catch myself slipping into old patterns, I didn't punish myself. I observed. I corrected. I would pause and say, That's an old thought. It has no authority here. And I would replace it. Not with empty affirmations, but with believable upgrades. I didn't say, "I'm a millionaire." I said, "I am building value and attracting what matches it." I didn't say, "I have it all together." I said, "I am learning, and I am further than I was."

Small shifts. But powerful.

Because belief is like a thermostat. You can only rise to the level you've set. And if your inner dialogue is cold, no amount of external motivation will keep you warm.

I remember a conversation with a close friend who asked, "How did you shift your confidence so deeply? You used to second-guess everything." And I smiled. Because it wasn't an overnight shift. It was a daily discipline. I had stopped arguing for my limitations. I had stopped seeking permission. I had stopped waiting for validation before thinking higher thoughts.

And the results were undeniable.

My relationships changed. I no longer tolerated shallow interactions. I wanted depth, truth, presence. I asked better questions. I shared more freely. And in doing so, I attracted people who mirrored those values.

My work changed. I became more focused, more creative, more willing to risk. I stopped hiding behind over-preparation. I trusted what I already knew and allowed intuition to guide what I didn't.

My health improved. Not just physically, but emotionally. I felt less anxious, less fragmented. The fog lifted. Clarity returned.

Because when your mindset is magnetic, it becomes a filter. It repels what no longer serves. It attracts what matches your new frequency.

This is not mystical. This is neurological.

You can literally change the structure of your brain through sustained thought. Neuroplasticity proves it. Repetition reinforces it. Stillness accelerates it.

And the subconscious becomes your ally.

It begins to echo your new thoughts. It stops dragging you back into old fears and starts helping you find evidence of your new beliefs. You look in the mirror and see someone you respect. You make a decision and trust it. You enter a room and do not shrink. That is magnetic living.

My Reflection:

You are always attracting. The only question is: are you attracting from fear or from freedom?

Your mindset is not a trend. It is a compass.

If you want different outcomes, you need different inputs. Not just externally, but internally. What you feed your mind, the images you dwell on, the emotions you entertain - they all send signals. They all build pathways. They all tell your subconscious what to recreate.

So choose wisely.

Speak kindly to yourself. Think with intention. Observe the old thoughts and gently replace them with new ones. Not because you're broken, but because you're building.

Build with care. Build with clarity. Build from truth.

And soon enough, the life you once imagined will no longer be a dream. It will be a reflection - of the mindset you chose to hold.

Legacy in the Small Things

"Offering kindness in daily life is a legacy of grace."

What if the things you think no one sees are the very things that define you most?

Legacy is so often imagined as something loud, enduring, and public - buildings named in your honour, books published, awards won, lives changed in sweeping, cinematic gestures. But often, the truest legacies are not forged in grand moments. They are etched, quietly and consistently, in the smallest acts. The ones done with no applause. The ones no one posts about. The kind look. The gesture of patience. The decision to stay calm when irritation is justified. These subtle, often unconscious moments form the emotional residue you leave behind in the lives of others. And what a powerful residue that can be.

I used to think that if I wanted to change my life, or someone else's, it would have to be through a bold move - some major declaration, or a huge shift in lifestyle. But over time, and especially through the practice of stillness, I learned that the most lasting changes began not with revolution but with a choice. A pause. A breath. A shift in the tone of my voice. A cup placed gently on a bedside table without being asked. The moment I caught myself before responding in sarcasm. These became the turning points. And they didn't just change me. They shifted the entire environment around me.

Brian Tracy teaches that true integrity is when your behaviour matches your values, even when no one is watching. He explains that the greatest influence we have isn't in our lectures or our advice, but in the consistency of our actions. And the subconscious records that consistency. It watches you when you are tired. It listens to your tone when you're under pressure. It stores what you rehearse. And what you rehearse becomes your reality. These small moments - the way we treat a waiter, the time we take with a child, the eye contact we hold with someone in pain - they leave marks. Even if they're never acknowledged, they live on in the neural pathways of others. And more importantly, in your own.

One moment that stays with me wasn't dramatic at all. I was walking back to my car in a car park, groceries in hand, mildly irritated by something unimportant. An elderly man was slowly pushing his trolley to the return bay. I took it from him, nodded, and walked it back for him. He barely reacted. Just a slight nod. But as I walked away, a strange warmth settled over me. Not because I had done something extraordinary. But because I had noticed. And in that act of noticing, I had reminded myself who I wanted to be. That one act softened something in me. And my subconscious registered it. That's how kindness works. Not as a show. But as an internal calibration.

Dr Joe Dispenza talks about coherence - when the heart and mind operate in alignment. When our energetic field matches our intention. He describes how people can sense when we are in coherence even if they can't explain it. It's not something you can fake. And it's certainly not something that happens accidentally. Coherence is a byproduct of practice. Of choosing small kindnesses until they become your default.

When you are in coherence, others may not remember exactly what you said, but they'll remember how they felt in your presence. They'll remember the peace, the steadiness, the quiet way you saw them. That's legacy - not what you leave behind, but how you live while you're still here.

After the end of my second marriage, the house became a quiet place. Sometimes painfully so. I was surrounded by the residue of absence. No conversations echoing in the hallway. No laughter behind the kitchen door. It was in that silence that I learned just how powerful small gestures could be. A text from a friend asking nothing in return. A cup of coffee delivered with no words. A long hug that didn't rush. In those moments, I felt human again. And not because someone solved my problems, but because they stayed present. It taught me a lesson I now carry into every relationship: people don't need your solutions. They need your stillness. Your calm. Your conscious awareness.

In The Spirit of 31, I explored the significance of timing and meaning during pivotal life crossroads. That book grew from the realisation that sometimes, we're not called to do more, but to notice more. The number 31 began showing up for me at a time when I was questioning everything. And instead of dismissing it, I paid attention. It became a subtle invitation to deepen my awareness, to find meaning not in major revelations, but in ordinary days. That's what legacy is too. It's the choice to invest fully in the here and now. To give your energy to the moment in front of you rather than chasing some far-off ideal.

Legacy is not something we construct in one stroke. It's something we live into with each small choice. The decision to be gentle. To apologise when necessary. To listen without planning a response. To refrain from gossip when it would be so easy to join in. These moments are like drops of water falling steadily into the reservoir of your subconscious. Over time, they shape who you are. They shape how others experience you. And long after the moment is gone, the energy of it remains.

There's an old saying, "Character is who you are when no one is watching." But I'd add something more. Legacy is who others become because of how you were when they were watching. Not your accomplishments, but your atmosphere. Not your words, but your example. Does your presence make people feel calmer, safer, more grounded? Do your small daily choices teach others what it means to be whole? That is the inheritance you offer the world.

You don't need to be famous to leave a mark. You just need to be faithful to the moment. To trust that a smile matters. That a pause before speaking matters. That how you show up at the kitchen table, the staffroom, or the supermarket checkout lane - matters. These tiny moments carry the weight of your whole being. And when offered sincerely, they create ripples that extend far beyond what you can measure.

So pause, and ask yourself - not what do I want to be remembered for, but how do I want people to feel in my presence right now? How do I want my children to remember my mornings? My partner to remember my evenings? My colleagues to remember our Monday mornings? These aren't sentimental reflections. They are instructions to your subconscious. They shape the narrative of your life, one gesture at a time.

You don't need a podium to matter. You don't need a plaque to be significant. You only need to be awake to the small things. And to trust that they are enough.

Because in the end, the most powerful legacy is often whispered, not shouted. Felt, not framed. Let your small things speak. Let them echo long after you've left the room.

Let them become your legacy.

Listening Without Defending

"Receiving correction with humility leads to peace."

What if the greatest block to your growth isn't ignorance, but defensiveness?

Most people do not listen. They prepare to respond. They armour themselves, even when no attack is coming. They hear feedback not as a mirror but as a threat. And in that moment of tightening, something crucial is lost. Growth is silenced. Connection is severed. The subconscious mind, which longs for truth and coherence, is instead fed a story of survival: protect at all costs. Even if it costs the relationship. Even if it costs your evolution.

Listening without defending is not weakness. It is one of the highest forms of strength. It signals to your subconscious that you are safe enough to be honest, to be open, to be seen. And only in that openness can transformation begin.

I remember clearly the first time I saw my own defensiveness not as a justified reaction, but as a learned reflex. A simple comment from a colleague had triggered me. They had questioned my teaching method - not harshly, just curiously - and I felt something tighten in my chest. I heard myself explaining, justifying, listing the reasons why I had done what I did. And then I watched their face shut down. The curiosity faded. Connection lost.

It wasn't their feedback that damaged the moment. It was my defence.

Later that evening, sitting in silence with my journal, I traced the moment back. Why had I reacted that way? What belief had been triggered? And what I found, beneath the words, was fear. Fear of not being good enough. Fear of being wrong. Fear of being seen without the armour I had worn for so long. And that fear had trained my subconscious to see any correction as danger.

But that was an old script. And it no longer fit the man I was becoming.

Brian Tracy teaches that your response to feedback determines the speed of your growth. Those who listen with grace accelerate. Those who defend, delay. I had been delaying for years without realising it. I had confused being right with being respected. I had misunderstood correction as rejection.

So I began the slow work of unlearning.

Dr Joe Dispenza often speaks of how the body becomes the mind. How we rehearse emotions like anger, resistance, and pride until they become our personality. Listening without defending, then, is not just a mental exercise. It is physical. You must learn to breathe through the tension. To relax your jaw. To drop your shoulders. To stay soft when everything in you wants to harden. This is how you reprogram the subconscious - not just through thoughts, but through presence.

It became a daily practice. Not just in professional settings, but at home. With my children. With friends. With myself. I began noticing the impulse to defend even in small moments: when my teenage son questioned a rule, when a friend misunderstood my intention, when my own inner critic whispered doubt. And I learned to pause. To stay open. To ask, instead of explain. What are they really trying to say? What part of me feels unsafe? Is there something here I can learn?

Over time, something miraculous happened. The fear began to dissolve. Not because I became perfect, but because I became present. My identity was no longer hooked to being flawless. It was hooked to being real.

In Shadow Work Evolution, I explore how defensiveness is often a mask for deeper shame. We block feedback not because we are arrogant, but because we are afraid of what it might confirm. That we are not enough. That we are too much. That we are unlovable. But none of those things are true. They are echoes. Leftover scripts from moments we haven't yet healed. When you do the shadow work, you create space between stimulus and response. And in that space, you choose. You become the parent of your own mind. You teach it: we are safe now. We can listen.

Cal Newport reminds us in his work on deep focus that clarity emerges not just from information, but from reflection. Listening without defending is an act of deep focus. You aren't scanning for attack. You are holding stillness. You are allowing yourself to be taught. And the subconscious, when bathed in that energy of humility, begins to soften its defences. It stops bracing for the worst. It starts looking for the truth.

There's one moment I return to often. It was during a difficult conversation with someone I love deeply. They were hurt. And they were naming things I had done - things I hadn't seen clearly, things I didn't want to believe about myself. In the past, I would have shut it down. Corrected their version of events. Defended my intentions. But that day, I did something else. I breathed. I kept my eyes soft. I said, "Tell me more."

What followed wasn't easy. But it was healing. Not just for them, but for me. Because in their truth, I found my blind spot. And in my listening, they found relief. That moment was a turning point. It rewired something fundamental in my nervous system. I saw that humility is not humiliation. It is liberation.

The subconscious mind, much like the people we love, responds to safety. When you stop attacking yourself, when you stop resisting input, when you stay open in the face of discomfort, your subconscious begins to recalibrate. It no longer sees correction as punishment. It sees it as guidance. A map to your next level.

Eulogy Writing was born from this realisation. That when we are gone, people won't remember us for being right. They will remember how they felt around us. Whether they could be themselves. Whether they felt seen. Whether we could apologise. Whether we made room for their truth. Writing eulogies taught me to live with that end in mind. Not morbidly, but mindfully. If today were my last conversation, would I want to leave it defended, or connected?

Listening without defending is legacy work. It is relationship repair. It is subconscious reprogramming at its most intimate. And it is something anyone can do, starting now.

    i.   Pause.
    ii.   Breathe.
    iii.   Soften.
    iv.   Listen.

The next time someone offers correction, or disagreement, or even just a different viewpoint, see it as a doorway. Not a wall. Open it gently. Walk through it slowly. Thank them - even silently - for the mirror.

And most of all, thank yourself.

You didn't fight this time.

You listened.

And that changes everything.

Speak With Purpose

"Speaking what is timely and true is a blessing."

What if every word you spoke was shaping the life you live?

We often think of speech as communication, as a means of expression or persuasion. But speech is more than that. It is creative force. Every sentence we speak carries belief, memory, energy. Every conversation is either reinforcing a pattern or rewriting one. And what we say aloud teaches the subconscious what to prioritise.

Most of us do not realise how careless we are with language. We speak to fill silence, to seek validation, to avoid discomfort, to prove we are clever or informed. We answer questions we do not care about and offer opinions we do not believe. In doing so, we dilute the power of our voice.

But there comes a moment when you realise your voice is not just a tool. It is sacred territory. It is how your inner world touches the outer one. It is the bridge between intention and reality. And if you learn to speak with purpose, you begin to reshape not just the way others see you, but the way you see yourself.

I did not learn this through reading or theory. I learned it in the silence after tragedy.

More than thirty years ago, while still at university completing my Bachelor of Education, I lost my younger brother in a high-speed car accident. He was eighteen. Full of charm, mischief, laughter, and promise. One poor decision. One moment of reckless driving. And he was gone. Just like that.

There were so many questions left unanswered. So many conversations we would never have. The shock rippled through every corner of my being. One moment I was studying for exams and planning a future in the classroom, and the next I was writing a eulogy for my little brother. No one prepares you for that.

I can still remember the numbness. The way time lost all structure. People would speak and I would nod, but their words seemed far away, like echoes through glass. Everyone wanted to comfort, to say the right thing, but there is no right thing. Just absence. A silence that no language can soften.

And in that silence, I wrote. Not because I was brave or insightful, but because someone had to say something meaningful at his funeral, and somehow it fell to me. That eulogy became the hardest piece of writing I have ever done. I wept over each line, not because the words were sad, but because they carried the truth I could not say aloud in casual conversation.

It was in writing those words that I caught a glimpse of the subconscious power of language. Each phrase, each memory, each pause was more than remembrance. It was reassembly. A pulling together of fragments into something that resembled wholeness.

But I must be honest. In those years following my brother's death, I did not process it properly. I returned to my studies, to teaching placements, to assignments and expectations, but something inside remained untouched, unresolved. I kept moving forward on the surface, but beneath it all, I was adrift. I didn't use silence to face it. I avoided silence altogether. Instead of becoming more observant or reflective, I busied myself with proving I was fine. I buried the grief beneath responsibility, not realising it was quietly shaping the way I related to others and to myself. The voice that had helped me write his farewell disappeared into the noise of my striving. It would be many years before I was ready - or willing - to truly hear it again.

It wasn't until much later, when I began practising sustained silence as a daily discipline, that I could finally revisit the language I had written that day with clear eyes. I realised I had not just eulogised my brother. I had started to eulogise an old version of myself - one who had not yet understood the gravity of what it means to speak from truth.

Brian Tracy reminds us that "clarity accounts for probably eighty percent of success and happiness." In speaking, clarity is not simply about being articulate. It is about alignment. Are the words coming from your core? Or are they echoes of someone else's expectations?

Dr Joe Dispenza adds another layer. He teaches that our words reinforce neural pathways. Every time we speak from stress, drama, or false identity, we deepen the grooves of that pattern. But when we speak from presence, when we speak what is true, timely, and essential, we start to wire new outcomes. The subconscious listens closely when we speak. Especially when we speak with emotion. It does not care whether the words are helpful or harmful - it simply records and obeys.

That is why idle speech is so dangerous. Casual negativity. Sarcasm. Self-deprecation. These might seem harmless in the moment, but they leave an imprint. They become part of the inner script. And once that script is embedded, we live it.

In contrast, speaking with intention invites healing. I remember working with a colleague who always prefaced her opinions with, "This probably sounds silly, but…" After a while, I gently asked her, "Why do you say that? Who told you your thoughts were silly?" She paused. Then tears filled her eyes. "My dad. Every time I tried to explain something, he'd interrupt and laugh."

That pattern had followed her into adulthood, into meetings, into relationships. She had internalised it so deeply that even her confident ideas arrived clothed in apology. But the moment she became aware of that language, she began to change it. "I've noticed I keep saying I sound silly," she said to me weeks later. "I don't want to do that anymore." And just like that, the rewiring began.

This is the subtle power of words. They become the environment your subconscious learns to live in.

Cal Newport's emphasis on "deep work" reminds us of the value of unbroken focus, but it also translates into conversation. Deep speech - language that is reflective, truthful, and considered - has become just as rare. In a world addicted to instant commentary and performative opinion, silence before speech is a radical act. It creates room for wisdom.

I began applying this principle in my classroom and my relationships. I stopped rushing to respond. I let questions hang in the air. I became comfortable with not knowing what to say straight away. And in that space, better words emerged. Fewer words, but fuller ones.

This shift transformed the way I taught, the way I parented, the way I moved through conflict. I was no longer reacting. I was responding - from a place of clarity, not compulsion.

The companion book to this chapter is Eulogy Writing. Not because every moment is a farewell, but because writing a eulogy teaches you what truly matters. What rises to the surface when all else falls away. In that book, I unpack the emotional, spiritual, and psychological weight of writing farewells - not just for others, but for ourselves. What version of you needs to be laid to rest? What outdated identity are you still speaking from?

Purposeful speech is not about eloquence. It is about essence. It is the ability to say what is needed without decoration or delay. It is also the courage to stay silent when nothing helpful can be said. And this is a form of mastery - not of language, but of self.

There is a blessing in restraint. The 38 Blessings name it clearly - "speaking what is timely and true." Not everything true is timely. And not everything timely is true. The wisdom is knowing the difference.

Your subconscious hears the words you whisper in the mirror. It hears the labels you place on yourself in frustration. It hears the private mutterings you offer when no one else is listening. And it believes them. If you want to change the beliefs that run your life, start by changing the way you speak to yourself.

Speak as if someone younger is listening. Someone vulnerable. Because they are - the version of you that still feels unworthy, unseen, unsure. Speak to them with clarity, with care. Say the words you never heard. Say them until they feel true.

And then, when you speak to others, speak as if your voice is painting the walls of their memory. Because it is.

    i.   This is not pressure. This is power.
    ii.   Speak with purpose, not perfection.

iii.   Speak with vision, not volume.

iv.   Speak only when your words will add to the moment, not just fill it.

Because words are not harmless. They are a contract with your subconscious.

And you are always listening.

Let It Hurt, Let It Heal

"Having insight into suffering is a higher blessing."

What if avoiding pain is the very thing keeping you from healing?

It is a cruel irony that in our pursuit of peace, we often run the fastest from the very thing that would give it to us. We avoid pain like a plague, pushing it down, talking over it, masking it with distractions that keep our hands full and our hearts numb. But pain is not the enemy. Unfelt pain is.

In the silent spaces I came to inhabit after years of overstimulation, emotional burnout, and personal loss, I discovered that pain has its own intelligence. It does not disappear when ignored. It waits. It waits for your stillness. It waits for your honesty. It waits for the moment you are quiet enough, brave enough, tired enough to finally stop outrunning it. And then, it begins to speak.

This chapter is about what happens when we stop resisting that voice.

There is no blueprint for suffering. It arrives uninvited and unprepared, without logic or fairness. I remember the weight of grief that sat on my chest when I lost my younger brother in a high-speed car crash. I was only in my early twenties, still at university studying for my Bachelor of Education. One moment I was planning lessons and assessments, and the next, I was standing beside a coffin, eulogising a boy who had been laughing only days before.

There was no time to process it properly. No silence. No tools. Only shock, questions, and a hollow numbness I didn't know how to navigate. I tried to be strong. I tried to carry on. But looking back now, I know that I did not grieve in the way my soul needed. I did not sit with my pain. I tried to reason it away. And that silence, that absence of true processing, became a locked room inside me for years.

Dr Joe Dispenza speaks about the emotional addiction to familiar pain. We think we are avoiding it, but really, we are living through it on repeat, reactivating the same chemistry over and over. Until we face it fully, the subconscious does not release it. We end up reacting to present moments with old grief. Our body remembers what the mind refuses to process.

Pain, when suppressed, becomes a template. It shapes how we love, how we trust, how we dream. I see this clearly now. I see how my own buried sorrow shaped the tone of my relationships, the way I responded to conflict, the distance I put between myself and certain emotions. It wasn't deliberate. It was protective. But it was also costly.

For years, I was emotionally efficient but spiritually exhausted. I could help others through their heartbreaks, but I had not yet walked my own with honesty.

Brian Tracy once wrote, "The only way out is through." And this applies not just to success or obstacles but to suffering itself. You cannot think your way out of pain. You must feel your way through it. With presence. With patience. With an open hand instead of a clenched fist.

Letting it hurt is not weakness. It is wisdom. It is allowing the wound to speak before it becomes a scar you no longer recognise.

I remember a night, not long after revisiting the loss of my brother in my silent practice, where I simply sat and let myself cry. No agenda. No fixing. No timeline. Just the raw ache of missing someone who should have had more years. I cried for his laughter, for the moments we lost, for the birthday he never reached. I cried for the boy I was, sitting in a pew in a black suit, too young to carry that kind of farewell.

And something shifted.

Not because the pain left. But because I finally met it with open arms. And in that space, something deeper emerged. Compassion. For him. For myself. For the way life sometimes cuts without warning.

That compassion became a salve. Not instant. Not miraculous. But real.

Cal Newport, though better known for his work on focus and productivity, often writes about the importance of solitude as a place for depth and clarity. In one of his reflections, he emphasises that uninterrupted time is not just for output but for introspection. In silence, our inner architecture becomes visible. And in visibility, we gain the ability to rebuild.

The subconscious processes pain differently when we are not pushing it away. It integrates. It understands. It rewires. I saw this in my own behaviour, gradually softening toward things that used to trigger me. I found myself more patient, more present, more willing to listen without rushing to problem solve. The healing was subtle, like light filtering into a darkened room. But it came. And it stayed.

The companion reading for this chapter is 365 Days of SOUL: Light in the Layers. That book is filled with daily reflections, but it is in the moments of grief and shadow that some of the most honest pages were born. The writing was not aspirational, it was necessary. I needed words to meet the heaviness I could not speak out loud. In those quiet mornings of journaling, a strange peace returned. Not because I had moved on, but because I had moved through. The light did not replace the darkness. It wove into it.

That same principle applies to healing. When we let the pain speak, we allow it to teach. When we write it, speak it, or sit with it, we transform it. Not into joy perhaps, but into wisdom.

People often ask me how long grief lasts. My honest answer is that it doesn't end. It evolves. You carry it differently. It becomes a quieter companion, less intrusive, more like a shadow that walks beside you rather than over you. And in that companionship, there is grace.

Healing is not forgetting. It is remembering with less resistance.

There is something deeply human about suffering that is acknowledged. It opens the heart in ways that perfect circumstances never can. It teaches empathy. It breaks down the illusion of control. It shows us that we are all, in some way, walking each other home.

I once thought strength meant never breaking. But now I understand that real strength is breaking open, not apart. Letting life shape you without shutting you down. Letting the tears come without apology. Letting the sorrow have its say without rushing it off stage.

And when you do this, when you finally let it hurt without resistance, something else quietly slips in. Healing. The slow return of breath. The softness that follows the storm.

My Reflection: If you are hurting, don't rush to mend. Don't mask it with busyness or drown it in noise. Let it be what it is. Sacred. Personal. Human. Grief is not a detour. It is part of the path. Pain is not proof of failure. It is the body's way of processing what the heart cannot carry alone.

And healing is not something you chase. It is something you allow.

Sit. Feel. Remember. Release.

Let it hurt. Then let it heal.

The Other Voice

"Clarity in hearing the truth is a supreme blessing."

What if the voice you've been ignoring is the one that already knows the answer?

There is a quiet voice that lives beneath the noise of the everyday mind. It is not loud. It does not fight for your attention. It speaks without urgency, without panic. It does not shout over your anxieties or debate your logic. It waits. It waits for the silence that so few of us ever create. And when it speaks, it sounds like clarity.

I used to think this voice was imagination. Or intuition. Or perhaps the lingering echo of someone else's wisdom I'd once read or heard. But the more I returned to stillness, the more I came to realise this voice had always been mine. Not the me that reacts, performs, or pleases, but the deeper me - the one that exists beneath identity, role, and expectation. This is the other voice. And learning to hear it has changed everything.

It did not arrive with fanfare. It came quietly during long walks without my phone, in the empty space between thoughts during meditation, in those rare moments when I wasn't trying to solve anything or impress anyone. At first, I only caught glimpses. A word. A knowing. A sudden moment of calm in the midst of an emotional storm. It never argued or explained. It simply felt true.

Dr Joe Dispenza speaks about coherence - when the heart and brain align, when we are not in contradiction with ourselves. He teaches that this state of inner harmony allows the subconscious to become a channel rather than a container. I didn't understand this at first. But over time, as I practised silence, I began to notice when I was aligned and when I was not. The other voice only arrived when I was in coherence. When I was present. When I was listening.

And it was always right.

The challenge, of course, is that the other voice is not the only voice in our minds. There is the voice of fear, loud and rehearsed. The voice of doubt, always second-guessing. The voice of comparison, fuelled by social input and past insecurity. The voice of our parents, our teachers, our critics, our culture. These voices do not come from within, even though they now live there. They are echoes of conditioning. And unless we learn to discern, we confuse their noise for truth.

This was my experience for many years. Even as a seasoned educator, someone trusted for guidance and wisdom, I was often drowning in internal commentary that did not belong to me. I would hear myself say yes when I meant no. I would follow paths that looked right but felt wrong. I would keep silent when something deep in me wanted to speak. I was performing alignment. But I wasn't living it.

It wasn't until I created enough stillness that I began to sense the difference. The other voice - my voice - always brought calm. It never reacted, it responded. It felt grounded, even if it led to hard choices. And when I followed it, I never regretted the outcome, even if it cost me comfort or approval.

This shift became most evident during a pivotal moment in my career. I was offered a leadership role - one that many would consider a step forward. On paper, it was perfect. Respect, recognition, increased salary. But every time I sat with the decision in silence, I heard the same inner whisper: not this. It wasn't fear. It wasn't sabotage. It was clarity. The role would have taken me further from what I valued - meaningful teaching, deep connection with students, creative space. It would have cost me my inner alignment.

So I declined. It was not easy. Some colleagues didn't understand. I was questioned, even criticised. But inside, I felt more certain than I had in years. The other voice had spoken, and I had finally listened.

Brian Tracy reminds us that successful people make decisions based on values, not pressure. That clarity is not a product of thinking faster but of thinking from the right place. When you align with your values, your decisions gain authority. And your subconscious stops fighting you. It starts assisting you.

The companion reading for this chapter is 365 Days of SOUL: Unveiling the Unknown. This volume came from a place of deep listening - each reflection an attempt to capture what rises when the ego sleeps and the soul speaks. Writing it was not a display of wisdom, but a practice of paying attention. I was not teaching - I was recording. Documenting the guidance that arrived in the quiet hours before the world awoke.

And that is what the other voice requires. Attention. Not control. Not analysis. Just presence. And trust.

Cal Newport writes about the cognitive residue that builds up when we fragment our focus. Each shift in attention, each input we absorb, makes it harder to return to depth. This applies not only to work, but to self-awareness. If we are constantly switching contexts - emotionally, mentally, spiritually - we never reach the depth required to hear the other voice. We stay in the shallows. We hear only the loudest internal voices, not the truest one.

To hear the other voice, you must create space. That may mean saying no to good things. Disconnecting from distractions. Leaving conversations that steal your energy. Creating rituals of stillness that are as non-negotiable as brushing your teeth. It may mean being misunderstood, because the world respects noise more than nuance.

But clarity has a frequency. And it can only be heard in quiet places.

There is a line I return to often in my journal: I will not live a life that silences my soul. It reminds me that every yes I give must be rooted in alignment. That success without integrity is a form of self-betrayal. That the other voice, once trusted, becomes the most reliable compass I will ever have.

My Reflection: If you are waiting for a sign, this might be it. Not my words, but your response to them. That subtle shift in your body. That nudge. That quiet knowing rising up as you read. Listen. Trust it. That is the other voice.

And it already knows.

The Pause Between

"Patience under pressure is a blessing that protects."

What if your most important transformation is not found in doing more, but in waiting well?

There is a space that exists between the old and the new, between the no longer and the not yet. It is the pause between. A sacred, often uncomfortable place where the next step has not yet appeared and the old life is already dissolving. Most of us rush through this space, trying to fill it with answers, action, distraction. But in doing so, we miss the very gift it holds - alignment, healing, and clarity that cannot arrive until we stop moving.

This chapter is about that pause. And how it saved me.

I have spent long stretches of my life in that uncomfortable space. After my second divorce, after the loss of my brother, even in the quiet endings of roles, friendships, and seasons of identity that no longer fit. These transitions were not marked by big announcements or clear roads. They were marked by silence, confusion, waiting. A time when it felt like life had paused, but the pressure hadn't.

At first, I resisted it. I wanted resolution. I wanted clarity, closure, certainty. I would keep myself busy, hoping to outrun the discomfort. But the longer I avoided the pause, the more exhausted I became. Nothing shifted until I surrendered to the space itself.

Dr Joe Dispenza often speaks of the "quantum void" - a space of nothingness from which new realities are born. He teaches that when you're no longer creating from memory, and not yet reacting to the external world, you enter a space of pure potential. It is uncomfortable because it is unfamiliar. But it is here, in this unknown, that the subconscious can reorganise itself.

I began to understand this during a time when every part of my identity felt under review. As an educator, a father, a partner, even as a writer, I felt a sense of dismantling. The roles were still there, but my connection to them felt different. I wasn't sure who I was becoming. And that scared me.

But instead of filling the void, I chose - for the first time - to wait.

Each morning, I would rise and sit. Not to meditate in a formal sense, but to simply be present with whatever showed up. I didn't seek insight. I didn't chase productivity. I just let myself exist in the space between the ending and the beginning. And something shifted.

The mind, when no longer forced to produce answers, begins to reveal truths. I started to notice emotional echoes I hadn't processed - small, buried moments of grief, frustration, regret. But I also began to feel something else. Spaciousness. A strange kind of inner calm. It wasn't happiness, but it was grounding. As if life was slowly reconfiguring itself beneath the surface.

Brian Tracy teaches that the subconscious needs time to integrate new ideas, and that clarity is often the product of stillness rather than speed. I found this to be undeniably true. In silence, between one version of myself and the next, I discovered not just who I was - but who I no longer needed to be.

The companion reading for this chapter is 365 Days of SOUL: Light in the Layers. That volume was born out of my deepest personal winter. Each daily reflection became a light I placed along the path while walking in darkness. I wasn't writing from mastery. I was writing from the pause. From the in-between. And in doing so, I created a mirror for others moving through similar transitions.

Cal Newport speaks of the cognitive benefits of deliberate rest - how true depth can only emerge from intentional disengagement. In a world obsessed with hustle, we forget that soil needs fallow seasons. That healing requires emptiness before renewal. That clarity needs space to land.

One morning, in that quiet pause, I had a vision of a bridge. I was standing on one side, with the past behind me, and the future hidden in fog. I couldn't see where the bridge led, but I knew I had to keep walking, one slow step at a time. Not to rush, but to trust that the path would hold.

That vision stayed with me. Not as a revelation, but as a reassurance. That the pause is not punishment. It is preparation.

Many people fear the in-between because it feels like failure. The loss of momentum. The absence of definition. But what if the pause is the most intelligent part of your journey? What if it is your subconscious saying: I need time to rewire this? What if, in waiting, you are becoming?

I look back now and see that most of the pivotal shifts in my life didn't happen in action. They happened in stillness. In the days when I didn't know what to do. When I felt lost or stuck. Those were the moments when the subconscious had enough space to bring new insight to the surface. But only because I stopped filling it with noise.

There is power in the pause. It is the breath before speaking. The silence between musical notes. The exhale before birth. It is sacred.

My Reflection: You are not behind. You are not broken. You are in the pause. And the pause has a purpose.

i.   Do not rush it.
ii.   Do not numb it.
iii. Do not fill it with things that delay your healing.

Sit with it. Honour it. Trust that something is growing beneath the surface, even if you cannot name it yet.

Let the pause shape you.

The next version of your life depends on how well you wait.

Face What Follows You

"Understanding causes and consequences brings wisdom."

What if the thing chasing you is not something outside of you, but something you have refused to turn and face?

It is one of the strangest truths of the subconscious: the longer you run from a thing, the louder it becomes. It gains weight, mass, density, not because it is growing, but because your avoidance is feeding it. Like shadows stretching across a wall, these unseen forces become distorted until they feel enormous, unmanageable, otherworldly. But the moment you face them, something shifts. They shrink. They explain themselves. They even offer gifts.

This is not a chapter about fear. It is a chapter about what happens when fear becomes form. When the unspoken takes shape. When the formless ache of your past becomes a creature with a name, a face, a narrative. And perhaps most powerfully, a story you can now re-author.

During the darker parts of my healing journey, I found myself circling a question that had no words. Something was following me. I could feel it. Not in the external world, but in the quietest parts of my mind. I would sit in silence and feel the pulse of something uninvited. Not evil, not dangerous, just deeply misunderstood. It had no name at first, no distinct shape. Just a presence. A sense of being watched by something within.

For a long time, I mistook that feeling for anxiety. I believed it was just unresolved emotion, the residue of grief and guilt. But then I realised something unexpected. That presence was not my enemy. It was part of me. A part I had buried under years of survival and strength and shouldering too much.

So, I did something strange. Something entirely unexpected. I stopped avoiding it. I turned to face it.

And when I did, I met a creature. A mythical one, made entirely of memory and metaphor. And then another. And another.

That is how the book Mythical Creatures and Cryptids was born. It was not a planned project. It was a subconscious expression. A way for me to give language and image to the things I could not say directly. Each creature in that book represented something I had fought within myself. The dragon of rage. The banshee of grief. The shapeshifter of identity. The kraken of overwhelm. I gave them names because I needed to reclaim the power they had taken. I gave them stories because I needed to see how they had shaped mine.

It was not a book about folklore. It was a book about facing what follows you. And by writing it, I began to follow something else entirely - my truth.

Dr Joe Dispenza says that "what you resist, persists." But more importantly, he teaches that the subconscious does not distinguish between what is real and what is imagined. It responds to emotional truth. Which means that if you carry unresolved guilt, your mind will build a world around it. If you carry fear, your body will respond as though it is still in danger. If you carry confusion, your decisions will reflect that fog.

But if you face it, if you look directly into the heart of what haunts you, the landscape changes.

I remember one evening in particular. I had been sitting in silence for an hour, feeling restless, tight-chested, scattered. I had been writing about the Wendigo, a creature of hunger and isolation, known in legend for consuming what it loves. And in the middle of my notes, I wrote something that took my breath away.

"I have become the thing I feared - always needing, never full."

I put down the pen. I stared at those words. And I cried. Not because it was sad, but because it was honest. That was the gift of that creature. It gave me access to a truth I had avoided: that my restlessness was not about lack, it was about misdirected longing. I wasn't empty. I was just full of the wrong things.

This is the power of metaphor. It bypasses logic. It speaks straight to the subconscious. And it is the power of naming what follows you. Because once it has a name, you can have a conversation with it.

Brian Tracy speaks often about clarity as the cornerstone of success. He tells us that clarity begins with self-awareness. But self-awareness is not just about personality quizzes or goal setting. It is about knowing your emotional landscape. It is about understanding the creatures in your inner forest. The ones you tamed. The ones you feared. The ones you secretly fed.

When I started seeing my inner struggles as creatures, something softened. The shame lessened. The fear changed tone. These weren't demons to be exorcised. They were parts of me that had been misunderstood. Some were trying to protect me. Others were wounded. Some had lost their way. All of them had something to say.

And all of them wanted to be acknowledged.

In this way, the book Mythical Creatures and Cryptids became a map. Not of external folklore, but of internal transformation. Each creature represented a part of the journey. And through writing their stories, I began to write my own.

The subconscious is mythological by nature. It does not speak in spreadsheets or bullet points. It speaks in images, metaphors, dreams, symbols. This is why dreams often feel like strange riddles. This is why ancient cultures used stories to explain emotion. This is why children speak to imaginary friends when they are scared - because naming something gives it shape and shaping something gives you power over it.

Cal Newport talks about deep work as a path to mastery. But I have found that facing what follows you is a path to peace. It is how you stop running. How you stop pretending. How you make friends with the shadows instead of constantly trying to outrun them.

I often ask myself now, what creature is walking with me today?

Some mornings, it is the Hydra - too many tasks, too many voices, not enough breath. Other times, it is the Phoenix - something inside me burning to be reborn. Occasionally, it is the Minotaur - confusion in the maze of expectation.

But I do not fear them anymore. I greet them. I name them. And I ask what they need.

This process, this journey of giving form to the formless, has become one of the most healing things I have ever done. It has allowed me to look at myself with compassion. It has given me distance from my triggers. It has turned anxiety into insight, guilt into understanding, grief into wisdom.

And perhaps most importantly, it has given me back my creativity.

Because once the subconscious feels heard, it begins to offer gifts. It gives you metaphors. It gives you characters. It gives you stories that only you can tell. Not because they are fictional, but because they are emotional truths disguised as tales.

There was a point midway through writing Mythical Creatures and Cryptids when I realised, I was no longer writing a book. I was writing my freedom. Every page was a letting go. Every creature was a confession. Every entry was a mirror.

It was the first time in years I felt completely unburdened. Not because the past had changed, but because I had.

If you want to activate your subconscious, try naming the things that have followed you the longest. Give your fear a face. Give your guilt a character. Let your self-doubt wear scales or feathers or fur. Then sit with it. Talk to it. Ask it why it came. You may be surprised by the answers.

Final reflection: The things that follow you are not always enemies. Sometimes, they are the parts of you that were silenced too soon. The emotions you were never allowed to name. The pain that was too complex for words. So your subconscious turned it into myth.

You are not being chased. You are being invited. Invited to name, to face, to understand. And once you do, once you stop running, you might just find that what follows you was never trying to harm you. It was trying to lead you home.

Let the creatures walk beside you. Let them teach you what fear tried to hide. Because when you finally face what follows you, you do not just reclaim your power. You reclaim your peace. And perhaps, for the first time, you walk forward unafraid.

The Mirror Always Finds You

"Knowing oneself is a blessing that cannot be taught."

What if the person you've been avoiding is the one hiding in your reflection? What if the pain you blame on others is actually waiting for you inside your own gaze? These are not questions designed to unsettle you - though they might. They are invitations. And if you're ready to accept them, they lead somewhere honest, unguarded, and transformative.

There comes a point on every healing journey where you run out of people to blame. A moment when the stories you tell about your past, no matter how valid, begin to lose their emotional charge. You still remember what happened. You still honour the pain. But something inside shifts. The outrage cools. The narrative softens. And in its place comes a quieter voice - one that doesn't shout, but asks: What now?

This is the moment the mirror arrives.

The mirror is not always kind. It does not flatter. It does not twist the truth to soothe your ego. But it is always faithful. It shows you where you are. Not where you pretend to be. And the more you resist its gaze, the more persistent it becomes. You meet it in relationships, in silence, in conflict, in stillness. And eventually, you meet it in yourself.

I used to believe that introspection was enough. That if I read enough books, journaled my thoughts, analysed my behaviour, I would become immune to the sting of my own shadow. But the shadow is not conquered by analysis. It is only integrated through awareness. And that awareness is not intellectual. It is deeply emotional. Sometimes spiritual. And often inconvenient.

In Shadow Work Demystified, I wrote about the hidden scripts that shape our behaviour - the buried fears, the inherited beliefs, the shame we carry without ever naming. At the time of writing it, I thought I understood my own darkness. But the truth is, I was only beginning to scratch the surface. I was still filtering my self-perception through the lens of logic. Still trying to outthink my wounds.

Then came a stretch of life that forced me off the page and into the mirror. The mirror showed up in places I hadn't expected: my reactions to stress, the impatience I felt with people I loved, the envy I didn't want to admit, the judgements I cast silently on others. None of these made me bad. But they made me visible - to myself. And that visibility was the beginning of true inner work.

Dr Joe Dispenza describes the subconscious as the storehouse of all our past programming. It runs like a background operating system, quietly influencing every emotion, every decision, every belief. But here's what most people miss: that operating system doesn't upgrade until you face the parts you've labelled unlovable. It doesn't shift with willpower or positive thinking alone. It shifts with truth. With acknowledgment. With the courage to hold your gaze in the mirror when everything inside you wants to look away.

There was a season where I did look away. I was tired of the work. Exhausted from peeling back layers. I wanted ease, not excavation. I wanted comfort, not clarity. So I numbed. Not with substances or chaos, but with distraction. I filled my days with noise. Reorganised things that didn't need fixing. Made myself useful to everyone but myself. And yet, the mirror waited.

One day, during a quiet afternoon at home, I caught my reflection in the hallway mirror. Not a glance - a gaze. I stopped. Noticing the weariness in my eyes. The tightness around my mouth. The way I had unconsciously braced against the world. And it hit me, not as a thought, but as a knowing: I had abandoned parts of myself that still needed love.

That evening, I returned to a practice I had used years before: mirror work. A simple exercise, really. You sit. You look into your own eyes. And you speak. Kindly. Honestly. Not with flattery or performance, but with the intention to reconnect. It sounds absurd, maybe even indulgent, but I assure you - it is one of the most confronting things you can do.

Because there is no hiding in the mirror. It sees through your performance. It registers your flinches. It reminds you of the pain you've stored in your eyes and the stories you've etched into your body. But it also reminds you of something sacred: you are still here. Still becoming. Still worthy.

Cal Newport argues that clarity comes not from trying harder, but from working more deeply. Mirror work, in this context, is a form of deep work. It cuts through distraction and delivers you back to yourself. Not the version you curate for others, but the one who exists before the world got loud.

The subconscious loves the mirror because it speaks its language. Repetition. Emotion. Imagery. When you meet your own gaze consistently with love, you begin to rewrite the scripts buried beneath the surface. You begin to neutralise shame, not by avoiding it, but by embracing the self that felt it. And this is where healing moves from abstract to embodied.

In my own journey, the mirror helped me reclaim parts of myself I had disowned. The grieving son. The disappointed teacher. The man who doubted whether his voice was worth hearing. Each time I met those parts with compassion, something inside me softened. And in that softness, my subconscious recalibrated. Not instantly. But steadily.

One of the greatest lies we believe is that we must hide our wounds to be loved. That if we show our cracks, we will be discarded. But the mirror - and the subconscious - teach a different truth. That love begins where masks end. That integration is more powerful than perfection. And that wholeness is not the absence of darkness, but the willingness to hold it with grace.

I share all of this not as someone who has mastered the mirror, but as someone who respects it. I still flinch. I still avoid. But less than I used to. And that, to me, is progress.

So if the mirror finds you today - in a comment that stings, a memory that won't fade, a behaviour you can't justify - don't look away. Sit with it. Ask what it wants to show you. And trust that whatever rises is not here to shame you, but to free you.

Because in the end, the mirror is not your enemy. It is your most faithful friend. The one who never stops reflecting back the truth that healing begins not when we find someone to rescue us, but when we finally choose to see ourselves.

And when we do, the subconscious smiles. Not because it's been conquered. But because, at last, it has been seen.

Part IV – The Soul Beyond Self

Quiet Wins

"Being patient with difficulty is a noble blessing."

What if the reason you have not seen the breakthrough is because you are looking for it in the noise, when it has always lived in the quiet?

We are conditioned to value big wins. The promotions, the milestones, the applause-worthy achievements. We set our eyes on outcomes and chase them with a mix of urgency and anxiety, hoping that when we arrive, the noise within us will finally quieten. But the irony is that the deepest peace, the most profound transformation, does not come with fanfare. It comes in the small, almost invisible victories that happen quietly within. When you choose stillness over reaction. When you speak with care instead of anger. When you return to presence after being pulled by distraction. These are the quiet wins. And they are the foundation of a life lived in alignment.

There was a period in my life when I kept asking for signs. I was knee-deep in personal confusion, facing questions I couldn't articulate and wrestling with a sense of dissatisfaction I couldn't explain. I'd sit in the silence, hoping for lightning bolt clarity. But what I got instead were faint whispers. Nudges. Gentle corrections. At the time, they didn't feel like much. But looking back now, I see them as sacred. Every time I listened to those whispers instead of forcing an answer, I moved closer to truth. Not the kind of truth that needs to be announced, but the kind that needs to be lived.

Dr Joe Dispenza often speaks about coherence and the energy field we emit when our thoughts, feelings, and actions are aligned. He says the quantum field responds not to what we want, but to who we are being. That line struck something deep in me. I had been asking life for answers without adjusting my frequency. I was trying to fix the outside without anchoring the inside. The more I pushed, the more I felt adrift. But when I started honouring the small wins, the ones no one saw, the energy shifted. I no longer needed to strive in order to feel whole. I just needed to show up consistently in the direction of who I wanted to become.

There's something deeply sacred about recognising your own quiet growth. The day you realise that you didn't spiral after receiving criticism. The moment you notice that your breathing remained calm during a stressful conversation. The instant you caught yourself before falling back into an old pattern. These are monumental. Not because they are loud, but because they show your subconscious has changed its allegiance. It now sides with presence over panic. Awareness over avoidance. Healing over hiding.

I remember a particular moment during a staff meeting, years after I had begun this work. A heated discussion erupted, and the old me would have been eager to interject, to argue, to make sure my opinion was heard. But that day, I simply observed. I listened. And when I did speak, it was brief, clear, and kind. There was no need to dominate, no need to prove. I felt anchored. As I walked out of the room, I smiled quietly to myself. That was a win. No one clapped. No one noticed. But I did. My nervous system noticed. My subconscious took note. And that is what matters.

Brian Tracy calls this the accumulation effect. He teaches that small, consistent changes repeated over time lead to exponential results. Not just in productivity, but in character. He reminds us that we become what we practise. And most of us are practising something all day long, whether we realise it or not. The question is: are we practising reactivity, or are we rehearsing resilience? Are we reinforcing fear, or strengthening calm?

This is the essence of quiet wins. They are not achievements you can measure with metrics or display on social media. They are felt in the slow rewiring of your nervous system, the softening of your heart, the calming of your mind. They appear when you no longer dread silence. When you no longer need to be right to feel secure. When you no longer chase validation to feel seen.

In Shadow Work Evolution, I explore this transition in depth - the movement from reacting to integrating. The book was born not from mastery, but from observation. I began to notice that the most enduring changes in my own psyche came not when I fought my shadow, but when I became curious about it. When I invited it to speak, without judgement. The small internal dialogues, the moments when I said, "I see you," to a fear I used to deny - those were the milestones. They taught me that the subconscious is not trying to sabotage us. It is trying to protect us with outdated strategies. And only when we meet those strategies with patience can we invite the subconscious to evolve.

There was a chapter I nearly didn't include in that book. It was too raw. Too close. But it became the chapter most readers wrote to me about. It described a moment where I faced my own self-sabotage and didn't run. I stayed. I breathed. I didn't fix it. I just bore witness. That's all. And yet, in that moment, something rewrote itself inside me. That is the power of a quiet win. It doesn't just change how you feel. It changes who you are.

We must begin to honour the invisible victories. The decision to put down the phone when you could have numbed. The breath you took before answering that call. The way you held space for your child when they were angry, instead of matching their intensity. These things matter. They are not small. They are sacred. They are the seeds of a transformed life.

Your subconscious is always watching. It does not respond to what you say you want. It responds to what you repeatedly do. If your days are filled with chaos, conflict, and clutter, your subconscious builds a home in that energy. But if your days include moments of pause, kindness, presence, and truth, then it slowly begins to rewire itself for peace. That is why daily practice matters. Not as a discipline to master, but as a message to your inner world. A message that says: this is what we now prioritise. This is what we now believe.

There is a gentleness required here. You cannot force transformation. You can only nurture it. Like a gardener tending a quiet plot, you water, you remove weeds, you wait. You trust the process. You celebrate the small green shoots. And eventually, you look up and realise the entire landscape has changed.

So I offer you this: take inventory of your quiet wins. Not just the ones from this year or this month, but the ones from today. Did you listen more than you spoke? Did you breathe through the tension? Did you choose rest without guilt? These moments are the blueprint of your evolution.

And if you feel like the change is too slow, like you're not progressing fast enough, let me remind you - stillness is a speed. It is the pace of sustainable growth. It is the rhythm of the subconscious healing. It does not shout. It does not hurry. But it works. Always.

Let your next step be quiet. Let your next win be internal. And let your life, over time, become a tapestry of these subtle, sacred shifts. That is how change becomes permanent. That is how you activate the subconscious - not with pressure, but with presence.

That is how you win quietly.

Mirror Moments

"Recognising one's own faults is a path to awakening."

What if every difficult person in your life was just a mirror, silently asking you to meet the part of yourself you've hidden?

There is a strange alchemy to the subconscious. It speaks in symbols, memories, sensations, and - most painfully - reflections. You will know it is working when life begins to place people in your path who evoke reactions you cannot immediately explain. Irritation. Jealousy. Frustration. Even awe. These responses are not random. They are invitations. Each one holds a key to a part of yourself you have not yet claimed.

In psychological terms, Carl Jung called this the shadow. Not because it is evil, but because it is unseen. The shadow is not the villain within you. It is the disowned potential, the shamed fragments, the tender wounds you were taught to hide. And like all unclaimed parts of the psyche, it does not remain quiet forever. It appears in the mirror. Not the one hanging in your hallway, but in the eyes and behaviours of others. This is why some people seem to trigger us more than others. They are revealing us to ourselves.

Dr Joe Dispenza explains that our subconscious programming influences how we perceive others. What we notice in them is often what we have repressed or overidentified within ourselves. He teaches that when we begin to rewire the subconscious, we notice a shift not only in how we feel, but in who we are drawn to and repelled by. Healing changes the mirror. When I first truly grasped this concept, it felt like the rug had been pulled from under me. I could no longer point the finger without three pointing back.

The first mirror moment I can recall with total clarity came during a team meeting at work. One colleague, known for being overly critical and abrupt, had just spoken in a tone I found deeply offensive. My body tensed. I felt judged, undermined, disrespected. I left the room in silence, boiling with indignation. But later, during a moment of stillness, I caught myself. Why did this bother me so much? Why was his opinion carrying so much weight?

And then it landed. His harsh tone mirrored my own inner critic - the voice I used on myself when I failed to meet my impossibly high standards. He wasn't attacking me. He was impersonating the way I attacked myself. That revelation stopped me in my tracks. The sting was real, but the source was not new. It had been with me for years.

That's the thing about mirror moments. They do not introduce new pain. They illuminate old wounds.

Brian Tracy once said, "The person we become is shaped more by the way we respond to adversity than by the adversity itself." When we see others as adversaries, we miss the gold. But when we pause, reflect, and ask what the reaction is showing us about ourselves, we open a doorway. It may not be comfortable, but it will be honest.

For much of my adult life, especially through the breakdown of relationships and the upheaval of divorce, I saw myself as the rational one. The steady hand. The peacemaker. And while that was often true, it was not the whole story. In moments of silence, I began to see the parts I had edited out - the need to control outcomes, the deep fear of emotional chaos, the way I would emotionally distance instead of confront conflict. None of these were done with malice. But all of them left an imprint. On me. On others.

It wasn't until I began working on Shadow Work Demystified that these fragments started to integrate. The book was more than a writing project. It was a reckoning. I had to face my own narratives; the stories I had rehearsed to avoid responsibility. And as I traced these patterns back to their roots - childhood beliefs, family dynamics, societal expectations - I found something both heartbreaking and beautiful. I had done the best I could with what I knew. But now, I could know more. I could see deeper.

That's the gift of the mirror. It reveals not just the hidden pain, but the hidden strength.

One morning, during a quiet walk, I recalled an argument from my first marriage. It had been a fairly benign disagreement about finances, but it had escalated quickly. At the time, I had blamed her tone, her logic, her timing. But as I walked in silence that day, a wave of understanding hit me. I had been afraid. Afraid of appearing incompetent. Afraid of being seen as a failure. That fear had morphed into defensiveness. And that defensiveness had killed the moment for connection. She wasn't attacking me. She was naming something I hadn't yet accepted in myself.

These reflections are not easy to sit with. But they are necessary if we are to rewire the subconscious. Because your subconscious does not care about your ego. It cares about truth. It will use whatever tools it can - people, patterns, even conflict - to show you where you are still split.

Cal Newport speaks often of deliberate practice as the foundation of mastery. In the realm of personal development, mirror moments are that practice. Every time you catch yourself reacting strongly to someone, and you pause to ask why, you are practising. Every time you shift from blame to curiosity, you are creating new neural pathways. And every time you own a piece of the shadow, you make more room for wholeness.

There was a student I taught years ago who challenged me in ways I wasn't prepared for. He was loud, defiant, impatient. My usual tools of engagement didn't work. I spent months feeling frustrated, even doubting my own abilities. But one afternoon, during a classroom reflection session, he said something that cracked my armour. He said, "You're the only teacher who doesn't pretend." I asked him what he meant. He shrugged. "You just are who you are, even when you're angry."

That comment stayed with me. It made me realise that what I saw as my failure - losing patience, showing my frustration - was, in his eyes, a form of honesty. He didn't need perfection. He needed presence. That student mirrored something I hadn't valued in myself - the willingness to be real. And from that day on, I taught differently. Not perfectly. But more openly.

Your mirror moments will not always arrive as dramatic scenes. Often, they whisper. A sideways glance from your child. A tightness in your chest after reading a social media post. A sense of envy when a friend shares good news. These are not signs that you are broken. They are signs that you are being invited deeper.

Because here's the truth. The people who trigger you the most may be the ones carrying your unclaimed traits. And the people you admire the most may be showing you what is possible for you too. Both are mirrors. Both are useful.

In Shadow Work Demystified, I wrote, "The integration of the shadow is not about changing who you are. It is about loving who you were too afraid to be." This still rings true. Your subconscious has no interest in shame. It wants coherence. It wants all parts of you to come home.

And that begins by paying attention to what life is showing you in others.

There is no shortcut for this work. It is ongoing. It requires humility, patience, and a willingness to feel uncomfortable. But it also brings the deepest rewards. Self-respect. Emotional maturity. The end of projection. And the beginning of inner peace.

The blessing that opens this chapter is perhaps one of the hardest to live - "Recognising one's own faults is a path to awakening." Not because fault-finding is noble, but because fault-acceptance is freeing. When you stop defending your image and start befriending your truth, the subconscious no longer needs to sabotage you to get your attention.

It starts to support you instead.

So let this be your practice. When something triggers you, pause. Ask, "What is this showing me about myself?" When someone's presence brings you joy, ask, "What is this awakening in me that I want to live more fully?" And when you find yourself alone, uncertain, and full of questions, look into the mirror with softness.

Because the answer you seek may not be out there.

It may be looking back at you.

Truthful Tides

"Speaking truth with grace is a noble blessing."

What if the truth you avoid is the very tide that will carry you home?

There are seasons in life when everything feels unsettled. The current beneath your feet begins to shift. Familiar ground turns to silt. And no matter how tightly you cling to the rocks of certainty, the water insists on movement. These are the moments when truth rises - not as a concept, but as a force. Something bigger than opinion, louder than fear. It does not shout. It swells.

Truth is not always comfortable. In fact, it is rarely easy. But it is always liberating. And when you begin to activate your subconscious, when you tune in to the deeper signals within, you can no longer pretend not to know. That inner knowing becomes a pulse. A wave you cannot hold back.

I felt the pull of this tide most strongly during the year my teaching career reached its third decade. By then, I had become well-versed in the language of leadership, system priorities, pedagogical frameworks. I knew how to navigate conversations, tick boxes, meet performance standards. But inside, something had started to fracture. It was not burnout in the traditional sense. It was deeper. A quiet ache, a longing for something more honest. I began to realise that much of what I had built was rooted in compromise. Not dishonest work, but safe work. Predictable. Polished. Polite.

But not always true.

Dr Joe Dispenza often speaks of coherence - the alignment between thought, feeling, and action. When we live out of alignment, the body suffers. The mind resists. The heart retreats. That was where I had found myself. Outwardly composed, inwardly dissonant. The subconscious was no longer willing to stay silent. It began to whisper in the pauses between meetings. In the early hours of morning. In the quiet moments walking between classrooms. And the message was simple - Tell the truth.

At first, I resisted. What would truth cost me? Would it be misinterpreted? Would it break things I had worked hard to keep together? But the cost of not telling the truth was greater. It was costing me my peace.

Brian Tracy reminds us that "honesty is the fastest way to prevent a mistake from turning into a failure." I had not made a grand mistake. But I had made a thousand small ones by saying yes when I meant no, by agreeing when I doubted, by staying silent when something important needed to be said. These were the waves I had held back for years. But tides always return.

Truthful living does not require you to expose every thought. It asks only that you stop abandoning yourself in moments that matter.

One afternoon, I was invited to contribute to a school-wide initiative - a programme that sounded impressive but felt misaligned with the needs of the students I knew best. Normally, I would have smiled, agreed, played the role. But this time, I paused. I spoke clearly. I said I believed we could do better, that we were missing something vital, that we needed to listen more to the learners rather than impose another structure. My voice shook. I worried I had overstepped. But as I looked around the room, I saw nods. One colleague whispered a quiet thank you as we walked out.

It had taken a small risk. But it made a big shift. I had stopped withholding myself.

These moments of speaking up are not always dramatic. Sometimes, they look like gently correcting a misconception. Sometimes, they look like walking away from a conversation that does not honour your values. Sometimes, truth is a sigh. A silence. A refusal to laugh at something cruel. A choice to sit with someone who is suffering. Truth is not performance. It is presence.

The companion reading for this chapter, 365 Days of SOUL: Unveiling the Unknown, is rooted in that same spirit. It is not about arriving at certainty. It is about living in alignment with what is emerging. The unknown is not your enemy. It is the place where truth incubates. When you stop needing every answer in advance, you begin to listen more deeply to the truths already stirring beneath the surface.

There is one particular passage in that volume that speaks of the tides of the soul. How they do not ask permission. How they rise unannounced, often at night, often in the quiet hours when the rest of the world is asleep. That was my experience during the months I began to confront my own inner incongruities. Old beliefs surfaced. Grief from years earlier found its voice. There were nights I would wake at 3 a.m., not in fear, but with clarity. Thoughts fully formed. Sentences that felt like guidance. Truth arriving uninvited, yet perfectly timed.

Cal Newport writes about "deep work" as the antidote to shallow living. I believe there is also such a thing as "deep truth" - the kind that does not change with opinion, the kind that anchors you. It is forged in silence. Sharpened by reflection. And it lives not in cleverness, but in courage. When I finally began to speak and write from that place, something shifted. Not just in my relationships, but in my sense of self. I was no longer trying to be understood. I was simply being truthful.

This is the turning point in the subconscious journey. When you realise that speaking truth with grace is not about winning arguments. It is about walking in peace. Your peace increases every time your inner world aligns with your outer actions. And your subconscious thrives in that clarity. You sleep better. You breathe deeper. You attract people who are not drawn to your performance, but to your presence.

I once read that every truth you refuse to speak becomes a weight you carry. And eventually, that weight changes your posture. It pulls your shoulders inward, clouds your gaze, stiffens your breath. I had known that posture. But I had also known the release. The lightness that comes when you finally say the thing you needed to say. Not with anger, not with ego, but with grace. That's what the Blessing for this chapter teaches - truth is not just what you say, but how you say it.

Speaking truth with grace is a noble act. Not because it draws attention, but because it draws integrity. When your words match your soul, the world begins to respond differently. You will notice less friction, less internal war. Not because everything outside changes, but because you are no longer at war within.

One of the most meaningful messages I ever received came from a former student. Years after I had taught him, he wrote to thank me. Not for what I had taught, but for how I had spoken to him. He said he remembered the day I told him, quietly, that I saw his potential even when he didn't. He said it changed the way he saw himself. I had forgotten the moment. But he had carried it.

That is what truthful tides do. They may begin with you, but they ripple far beyond.

Let me offer this My Reflection: Your truth is not a threat. It is a tide. It does not arrive all at once, and it does not need to drown anyone. But it will rise. And when you ride that tide - when you let your inner knowing shape your outer choices - you begin to live a different kind of life. One not ruled by noise, performance, or expectation, but led by clarity, anchored by grace.

So let your truths rise. Let them take their place in your words, your pauses, your decisions. You do not have to speak loudly. Only honestly. The tide will do the rest.

Soft Landing

"Having humility in daily life is a supportive blessing."

What if the lesson was never about how high you could climb, but how gently you could return to earth?

We often mistake the spiritual journey for a kind of ascent, a climbing upward into light, wisdom, transcendence. But real transformation is not just about elevation. It is about descent too. About integration. About how you land, how you return, how you carry the insight into the ordinary, the quiet, the overlooked. This is the soft landing. The return to self, to soil, to the sacredness of now.

When I first began my deep work practice, I had visions of clarity that felt luminous. Breakthroughs, stillness, vast inner space. And those were real. They came in silence, in solitude, in surrender. But the deeper work was not in the soaring moments. It was in the return. In doing the laundry with awareness. In replying to a difficult email without ego. In waking up early for my responsibilities without resentment. These are the places where enlightenment gets tested. Not in the retreat, but in the routine.

It was not until I began teaching again, after the most intense season of inner rewiring, that I truly saw the value of the soft landing. My classroom became a mirror. The students, a feedback loop. Their energy told me if I was carrying peace or performance. And I began to notice that when I entered the room with gentleness rather than intensity, everything shifted. The atmosphere softened. Behaviour problems lessened. Eye contact increased. Trust grew. Not because I had done anything radical, but because I had landed differently. I wasn't hovering above my life anymore. I was in it.

Dr Joe Dispenza talks about the integration of new neural pathways. That it is not enough to have an epiphany or a state of coherence. The body must learn the feeling. The routine must absorb the change. This, he says, is where change becomes reality. It is no longer a concept. It becomes how you live.

Soft landings are not passive. They are powerful. They require discipline, not just inspiration. The ability to return to the moment, again and again, without needing it to be glamorous. The willingness to tend to the ordinary with reverence. To breathe slowly while waiting in line. To speak kindly when it would be easier not to. To honour your tiredness without collapsing into complaint. These are small acts. But they are spiritual gold.

The day I finally understood this, I was not in a temple or a mountain or a meditation room. I was sitting in traffic. I had been delayed, missed a call, forgotten a document. My heart was tight. I felt the old current of frustration rising, the inner monologue ready to spiral. But then something stopped me. A still voice within said, You're safe. You're here. Just land.

And I did.

I looked at the sky. Noticed the clouds. Breathed through my nose. Smiled without forcing it. I was still late. But I was no longer lost.

This is the invitation of the subconscious. Not to escape the body or bypass the mess, but to meet it fully, lovingly, without resistance. To come home to yourself, again and again, no matter what the outer scene looks like.

In Sacred Stones, I wrote about the practice of stone stacking, a seemingly simple act that became, for me, a profound spiritual ritual. Each stone held a presence. A weight. A story. And the art of balancing one upon another without force became a metaphor for living. You cannot rush it. You cannot force it. You must feel, adjust, listen. And when the final stone lands softly, aligned and true, there is a quiet peace that floods your being.

That is how I want to live.

Not with noise, but with nuance. Not with performance, but with presence. Not with constant striving, but with the grace of a soft landing.

There was a moment during the writing of Sacred Stones when I was standing alone at a rocky riverbed. I had stacked a small formation by hand, breath steady, mind still. Just as I stepped back to admire it, a light breeze blew. The top stone wobbled, then fell. I laughed out loud. And instead of rushing to rebuild, I let it be. That too was a kind of soft landing. The acceptance of impermanence. The humility to let go of control.

The blessing in this chapter speaks of humility. Not humiliation, but humility. The sacred knowing that you are not above the moment, nor below it. You are part of it. You belong to it. And that real strength is quiet, grounded, gentle.

Brian Tracy reminds us that consistency is the hallmark of maturity. It is not the occasional burst of brilliance that shapes a life, but the steady, repeated acts of character. Showing up when it matters. Following through on your word. Listening more than you speak. Apologising when needed. These are the stones that build a meaningful life. This is the ground of the soft landing.

And yet, we are conditioned to seek the highs. The applause, the validation, the peaks of productivity or popularity. It takes real courage to slow down. To drop out of the performance race. To prioritise depth over display.

When I was younger, I thought my greatest contribution would come through what I said, what I taught, what I published. But now, after decades of inner work, I see that my true legacy may lie in how I listen. How I pause. How I make others feel safe to be themselves in my presence.

That is the work of the subconscious. It is not loud. It is not glamorous. But it is transformative.

There is an old saying that the way you do anything is the way you do everything. I have found this to be true in the most surprising ways. How I enter a room. How I tie my shoelaces. How I respond to a message. All of it carries an energy. And that energy, if cultivated with care, becomes a sanctuary.

So, this chapter is not a call to leap. It is a call to land.

To feel your feet on the floor. To let your breath move without management. To open your heart without agenda. To be still without needing a lesson. And to trust that this, exactly this, is enough.

You do not need to prove your growth to anyone. You do not need to dramatise your healing. You only need to return. Return to the quiet. Return to your breath. Return to the stone you are placing, the meal you are making, the child you are holding, the silence you are honouring.

This is how you know you are healing: you no longer seek the next mountaintop. You begin to find holiness in the valley. You begin to feel peace in the pause. You begin to land, softly, inside your own life.

Let this chapter be your invitation to soften. To slow. To settle. To come home, not just to what is beautiful, but to what is real.

The work is not finished when the breakthrough comes. It is finished when the lesson can be lived without performance. When it becomes who you are without effort.

That is the soft landing.

And that is where true transformation takes root.

From the Author's Chair

There is a moment in every long journey where you pause. Not because you are tired, but because you finally realise how far you've come. This is that moment.

When I began this work, I didn't set out to write a book about the subconscious. I was trying to survive the noise. I was trying to recover from a silence that had been forced upon me after loss, disappointment, and the kind of grief that doesn't come with answers. My life was not a carefully constructed narrative. It was a slow unravel followed by a quiet rebuild. What you've read in these chapters is not a formula. It is a reflection. A capturing of the years where I decided to stop performing and start listening.

At first, the silence felt like failure. I had spent decades in motion - teaching, fathering, learning, carrying responsibility like a badge. But beneath all that movement, there was a hollow ache. Something had been left unheard. And it was only in the silence, in the absence of performance, that I began to recognise its voice.

I remember the early days. Mornings when I would rise before the sun, not out of discipline, but because sleep would not come. Evenings when I would sit with a glass of wine and the unanswered question of who I had become. There was no audience. No applause. Just presence. I began to write - not to publish, but to empty. To spill what was caught between memory and regret. Slowly, the words became companions. They held space where conversation had failed. And I followed them. One page at a time.

As I watched myself on this journey, I could almost imagine a camera following my quiet movements. Not the grand scenes, but the in-between ones. The subtle shifts. The breath before I answered. The hesitation before I reacted. The blink of understanding when a pattern finally made sense. The Truman Show concept came to me during this time - not because I believed I was being watched, but because I had become the watcher. I had stepped back from the script of my life and started observing the director behind the scenes. That director, I realised, was my subconscious. And he had been trying to communicate for years.

This is not the kind of self-help journey that ends with a trophy or a revelation. It ends, instead, with a soft nod. A quiet agreement between parts of yourself that have long been at odds. The conscious mind, exhausted from effort. The subconscious, waiting patiently in the wings. When the two finally meet, what follows is not applause, but stillness. A knowing. A reunion.

The voices that guided me - Brian Tracy, Dr Joe Dispenza, Cal Newport - were never distant figures on a bookshelf. They became interior mentors. Their teachings echoed during my moments of doubt, reminded me to be deliberate with my time, my thoughts, and my energy. They gave language to what I had begun to feel but could not yet articulate. And more than anything, they reminded me that transformation is not an event, but a practice.

Many of the books I wrote during this period came not from ambition, but from necessity. Phobia Fighter helped me decode the grip of fear. Shadow Work Demystified gave me a map for the darker corners of myself. Eulogy Writing opened a doorway back to my brother, whose sudden death had left an ache I carried silently for decades. Sacred Stones helped me see the beauty in things placed with care. And the 365 Days of SOUL series gave structure to the whispers of clarity I received in the quiet hours of the morning.

These books are not separate from 'Activate the Subconscious', they are its extended breath. Its companions. Its echoes. Together, they trace the outline of a man coming home to himself.

Watching Myself from Above

If you had told me, back then, that I would one day write this book, I would have smiled politely and returned to my marking. I was a teacher. A father. A man living out his commitments. But I was not awake.

Now, when I look back, I see the signs. I see the moments I chose silence over conflict, depth over distraction, reflection over reaction. I see the younger version of myself, running from grief, burying the pain of losing a brother in a high-speed crash, pushing forward through the trenches of daily life without ever stopping to breathe. I see a man trying to be strong by staying busy.

And I see him begin to pause.

The transformation wasn't dramatic. It was found in smaller gestures. In handwritten notes to myself. In choosing stillness over scrolling. In long walks without a podcast. In choosing not to respond right away to provocation. In speaking to my children with a softness I had not been raised with. I watched myself become someone else - not through effort, but through allowing.

There is something deeply humbling about realising that the life you lived for so long was only a rehearsal. That the real performance begins the moment you stop pretending. That's what this journey has been for me. A quiet exit from the stage. A return to the wings. And from there, a renewed presence - rooted, open, and awake.

This book is my offering. Not as an expert, but as a witness. A witness to my own forgetting and remembering. A witness to the power that silence holds. A witness to the truth that everything we seek is already within us, quietly waiting for space.

If you have made it this far, then something in you is ready. Ready to trust your own rhythm. Ready to step out of the noise and into the deep current beneath it. Ready to listen. To observe. To become the watcher of your own life - not with judgment, but with grace.

You are not alone on this path. Your subconscious is with you. Always has been.

And so am I. In stillness and in strength,

Jason A. Solomon, B.Ed
From the Author's Chair 2025

Appendix

The 38 Blessings

(MahaMangala Sutta) Short interpretations and chapter markings identified with a ★

Foundational Wisdom (Sīla – Moral Foundation)

★ Not associating with fools
Avoiding negative influences protects your energy and subconscious stability. The people you avoid shape your growth just as much as those you embrace.

★ Associating with the wise
Wisdom is contagious in the company of those who live it. Your environment directly programs your subconscious over time.

★ Honouring those worthy of respect
Paying respect to teachers, elders, and guides anchors your soul in humility. This reverence reinforces your alignment with truth.

★ Living in a suitable place
The spaces you occupy influence your emotional climate. Peaceful environments help rewire inner chaos.

★ Having done good in the past
Past actions create stability beneath your feet. The seeds you've sown continue bearing fruit in the present.

★ Setting your mind in the right direction
The intention behind your thoughts is the blueprint of your life. Direction is stronger than speed.

Skill & Daily Life (Training Body, Speech & Mind)

★ Deep learning
Intentional learning reshapes the subconscious and awakens
dormant potential. What you study becomes what you notice.

★ Skill in profession or craft
Mastery of your vocation grounds identity and purpose. Your
craft becomes a mirror of your focus.

★ Disciplined conduct
Self-regulation deepens inner freedom. The ability to pause is
more powerful than the urge to react.

★ Kind speech
Your words create emotional blueprints in the minds of others.
Language is a vessel of energy.

Home & Relationship Harmony (Domestic Order)

Caring for parents
Respect for your roots strengthens your inner foundation.
Honouring where you came from supports where you're going.

★ Cherishing your spouse and children
Every small act of love within the home etches a legacy in the
nervous systems of those closest to you. Kindness at home is the
most enduring footprint.

★ Peaceful livelihood
Work that aligns with your values becomes part of your spiritual
practice. Stability without strain nourishes the soul.

Social Values (Giving and Right Action)

★ Generosity
Giving without expectation trains your subconscious for abundance. Generosity is the soul's exhale.

★ Living in line with Dharma (truth)
Living truthfully brings a quiet coherence. The more your actions match your values, the less conflict you feel.

Supporting relatives
Strong family ties bring emotional grounding. Connection is a subconscious safety net.

★ Blameless behaviour
Integrity creates subconscious calm. The less you have to justify, the more energy you save for growth.

Protection and Purity (Guarding the Mind)

★ Avoiding evil
Avoiding harmful behaviour preserves your inner alignment. What you reject becomes as defining as what you pursue.

Resisting temptation
Restraint becomes a superpower when used with clarity. Turning away from impulse strengthens internal will.

Refraining from intoxicants
A clear mind is a gateway to intuition. What fogs your senses disconnects you from your source.

★ Diligence in spiritual practice
Consistency in spiritual habits reshapes subconscious patterns.
Practice is where the sacred becomes real.

Mental Development (Samādhi – Cultivating the Mind)

★ Reverence
When you honour life's sacredness, life honours you back.
Reverence invites depth into the everyday.

★ Humility
Letting go of superiority invites grace. Humility opens doors that
pride locks shut.

★ Contentment
Gratitude for what is brings peace with what isn't. Contentment
stops the inner chase.

★ Gratefulness
Acknowledging your blessings changes what your subconscious
tracks. The more you thank, the more you notice.

★ Listening to Dharma at the right time
Hearing truth when you're ready transforms you deeply. Timing is
part of wisdom.

★ Patience
Patience is the nervous system's strength training. Waiting
without anxiety rewires urgency into peace.

★ Willingness to be corrected
Receiving correction humbly shows inner maturity. Every critique is a mirror if you choose to look.

Seeing noble beings (teachers/monks)

Being around awakened souls leaves subconscious imprints. Their energy speaks beyond words.

★ Discussing truth at the right time
Truth lands softly when the heart is ready. Meaningful conversation can reroute your entire path.

Wisdom and Awakening (Prajñā – Insight and Realisation)

★ Self-restraint and simplicity
Less allows more. Subtraction creates clarity.

Living a holy, chaste life
Sacred living protects your essence. Purity builds deep inner trust.

★ Seeing the Noble Truths
Understanding suffering opens the path to freedom. Insight clears emotional fog.

Realising Nibbāna (freedom)

True liberation is inner. It's a release, not an escape.

★ Unshaken mind in worldly changes
Steadiness in the storm is real power. Equanimity is a higher frequency.

Freedom from sorrow
Letting go of attachment heals generational pain. Joy grows in surrendered soil.

Freedom from defilements (passion and ego)
What no longer controls you no longer defines you. Lightness comes when need falls away.

★ Complete security
Peace is not the absence of threat, but the presence of inner anchoring. True safety lives within.

Companion Reading List

All book titles curated by Jason A. Solomon, B.Ed.

Each of these titles were written as a standalone journey - yet when paired with this book, they offer layered insight, deeper integration, and personal expansion.

📔 Shadow Work Demystified

Referenced in: Chapter 1, Chapter 21, Chapter 23

Explore the unconscious forces that shape our decisions and identities. This book offers a practical guide to integrating your shadow - the hidden aspects of self - through gentle self-reflection and emotional truth-telling.

📔 Phobia Fighter

Referenced in: Chapter 2

Uncover the roots of subconscious fear loops and learn to dissolve them with intention and awareness. This book provides tools for recognising how small fears shape big behaviours.

📘 Seeds of Stillness: 365 Days of SOUL

Referenced in: Chapter 6, Chapter 16

Begin your inner transformation with grounding, presence, and calm. This volume offers daily reflections centred on stillness - a quiet revolution for those beginning their soul work. Based in the element of Earth.

📘 Origins of Opening: 365 Days of SOUL

Referenced in: Chapter 16

Awaken layers of vulnerability, clarity, and growth through soulful writing prompts and elemental wisdom. Ideal for expanding your inner inquiry after stillness has taken root. Based in the element of Fire.

📘 Unveiling the Unknown: 365 Days of SOUL

Referenced in: Chapter 16

This volume challenges you to meet the hidden parts of yourself with curiosity and compassion. A spiritual invitation to welcome mystery as a guide. Based in the element of Water.

📘 Light in the Layers: 365 Days of SOUL

Referenced in: Chapter 18

A soul-deep practice of rediscovery through the daily mess and magic of life. A journey through healing, clarity, and conscious choice - one layered reflection at a time. Based in the element of Air.

📘 Eulogy Writing

Referenced in: Chapter 15

This book was written from the heartbreak of losing my 18-year-old brother in a tragic car accident. It invites readers to find healing, presence, and clarity through the sacred practice of writing in times of grief.

📘 Mythical Creatures and Cryptids

Referenced in: Chapter 19

A surprising doorway into the subconscious, this book helped me visualise my inner demons and give them form. What began as curiosity became catharsis - a deeply healing creative work masked in mystery.

📖 Shadow Work Evolution

Referenced in: Chapter 22

A follow-on from Demystified, this volume explores deeper layers of the shadow once stillness and inner space are established. Ideal for those moving from awareness to transformation.

📖 The Spirit of 31

Referenced in: Chapter 13

Written as a spiritual and numerological guide, this book reveals how angel numbers and repeated signs become part of our subconscious blueprint. A gentle companion for those sensing spiritual timing at play.

Acknowledgements

This book was born in the silence that followed years of noise.

To those who stood beside me in that silence - even when they didn't understand it - thank you. Your quiet support, your patience, your grace, allowed me to listen more deeply than I ever had before.

To my students across the decades - you were never just learning from me. I was learning from you. Every conversation, every spark of insight, every moment of stillness in a noisy classroom helped shape the work that now lives in these pages.

To the readers who found healing in my earlier books, thank you for walking this path with me. Your messages, your reflections, and your courage to face what is hidden became the silent chorus urging me to write this.

To Dr Joe Dispenza, Cal Newport, and Brian Tracy - your teachings met me when I most needed them. You lit torches for me when in the darkness, and I carried them into my own cave of the subconscious.

To my family - especially those no longer here - your memory lives in the quiet pauses between these lines. My brother, taken far too young, still speaks through the choices I make and the depth I now seek. I honour you not only in what I write, but in how I live.

To those who read this book and see themselves between the words - may it meet you where you are, and may it lead you home.

And finally, to the voice within - the one I silenced for too long - thank you for waiting. I hear you now.

With quiet reverence,

Jason A. Solomon, B.Ed.

The End